Cuddly Snuggly QUILTS

WITHDRAWN

LINDA K. JOHNSON & JANE K. WELLS

American Quilter's Society
P. O. Box 3290 • Paducah, KY 42002-3290
www.AmericanQuilter.com

Located in Paducah, Kentucky, the American Quilter's Society (AQS) is dedicated to promoting the accomplishments of today's quilters. Through its publications and events, AQS strives to honor today's quiltmakers and their work and to inspire future creativity and innovation in quiltmaking.

Executive Editor: Andi Milam Reynolds
Senior Editor: Linda Baxter Lasco
Graphic Design: Lynda Smith
Cover Design: Michael Buckingham
Photography: Charles R. Lynch, unless otherwise noted

Additional copies of this book may be ordered from the American Quilter's Society, PO Box 3290, Paducah, KY 42002-3290, or online at www.AmericanQuilter.com.

Text © 2010, Authors, Linda K. Johnson and Jane K. Wells
Artwork © 2010, American Quilter's Society

Library of Congress Cataloging-in-Publication Data

Johnson, Linda K.
 Cuddly snuggly quilts / by Linda K. Johnson and Jane K. Wells.
   p. cm.
 ISBN 978-1-57432-672-7
 1. Quilting--Patterns. 2. Patchwork--Patterns. I. Wells, Jane K. II. Title.
 TT835.J5853 2010
 746.46--dc22

           2010032617

Here are some of some of Linda's grandkids, Mackenzie, Piper, Taylor, and Griffin, playing and snuggling with their quilts.

Jane loves entertaining her grandkids. Can you imagine the fun they share at a sleepover when everyone cuddles up in their own quilt?

 American Quilter's Society
P. O. Box 3290 • Paducah, KY 42002-3290
www.AmericanQuilter.com

Proudly printed and bound in the
United States of America

Contents

General Instructions

About These Quilts

This is a wonderful collection of original quilts designed for our children, from tots to grown-ups. These are not your usual "baby" quilts, but rather exciting designs, each based on a particular child's personality and interests.

A major concern when making a quilt for a kid is that we don't want to put so much time into the quilt that we are disappointed when the child loves it to death. These are not meant as heirlooms, but fun quilts moms and grandmas can make for their kids and grandkids to enjoy and wrap up in as though we are giving them a big old hug!

Our patterns are more complicated-looking than they actually are to construct, partly because of value placement. All these patterns are beginner-friendly, but we offer several different techniques that will appeal to all skill levels. They include pieced circles, rocking squares without bias edges, whimsical raw-edge appliqué, the "no binding" finishing technique, and some new variations of pieced blocks.

Note: All strips are cut across the width of fabric unless otherwise specified.

Sizes

When you are making a cuddle quilt, you have the freedom of choosing any size you want because bed sizes are irrelevant. Sometimes the age of the child will help you determine the size. Do you want to wrap a baby, or provide a play mat for the baby to crawl on? Do you need a longer quilt for an older child to cuddle up with? Perhaps a full-size bed quilt is what you're looking for. All of the quilts in this book can be adjusted to fit the size that's right for you by increasing or decreasing the number of blocks and/or the number and size of the borders.

Finishing Your Quilts

Batting

We love the look, feel, and drape of low-loft cotton batting in our quilts. However, we recently discovered how much we also like using wool batting. It's still a natural fiber but it's loftier and denser than the thin cottons.

Backing

Your backing fabric should be at least 4" larger than the quilt top on all four sides. If you are using yardage that is not as wide as your quilt top, you will need to do some piecing. You can buy enough yardage of one fabric or piece together all your leftover fabrics from the quilt top. Another suggestion is to back cuddle quilts with soft, cozy flannel.

Layering and basting for machine quilting

Secure the backing to a table or floor with large binder clips or tape, keeping it slightly taut, but not stretched. Lay the batting over the backing, gently patting it smooth without pulling it. Lastly, lay the quilt top over the batting, making sure that backing and batting extend beyond the quilt top on all four sides. Use large rulers to check that your rows are straight and corners are square.

If you are pin basting your layers together, use rust proof, small (number 1) safety pins every 3"–4" for a small quilt (closer together for large quilts). Keep the top smooth and taut.

We replaced pin basting with spray adhesive basting on several of the small quilts. We love this technique because it saves hours of basting time. We use 3M Spray Mount™ Artist's Adhesive between all three layers. It holds the layers together well and does not harm the fabric. It works best to spray half of the quilt top at a time and have a friend help you smooth the layers out.

Binding

We prefer single-fold bindings because they are not as bulky and you can get really square corners. Choose fabrics that will enhance the quilt. You can use one fabric or several scraps. It doesn't necessarily

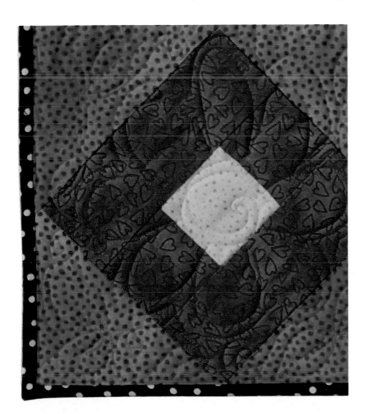

have to be a fabric that was used in the quilt top; this is your last chance to add color or design.

Cut binding strips on the straight of grain 1¼" wide. Leave an 8" tail at the beginning and start sewing away from a corner, right sides together. Sew a ¼" seam, stopping ¼" from the corner. Backstitch and remove the quilt top from under the needle. Flip the binding up at a 45-degree angle, then fold it down with the top fold at the edge of the quilt and the raw edge aligned with the next side to be sewn. Continue sewing around all four sides until you are about 10" away from where you started sewing; backstitch and remove the quilt from under the needle.

Trim binding ends at 45-degree angles, overlapping the length by ⅜". Sew the ends together with a ¼" seam and press open. Finish sewing the binding onto the quilt top.

Press the binding over the quilt edge. Turn the raw edge under until the fold just covers the seam line on the quilt back. Slipstitch in place by hand, or machine stitch in the ditch from the front of the quilt, making sure the fold of the binding is caught on the back.

Label

Don't forget to include a label on the quilt back. Include your name, city and state, the date you finished the quilt, and include the name of the person you made the quilt for and maybe even the occasion.

You can write the info on fabric with an ultra-fine point permanent marker, hand or machine embroider the info onto a label, or print it from your computer onto special fabric sheets you run through your inkjet printer. You may add borders or appliqués to the labels to jazz them up, or even include a photo. The labels should be hand stitched to the back of the quilt after the quilting is finished.

Cuddly Snuggly Quilts ☺ Linda K. Johnson & Jane K. Wells

Grandma Loves Braxton

40" x 50", designed, made, and quilted by Jane K. Wells for grandson Braxton

GRANDMA LOVES BRAXTON consists of 12 – 10" finished Log Cabin blocks set in straight furrows. There is a 1" inner border and a 4" outer border.

Fabric Requirements

Focus fabric: 1 yard for center squares or
enough to get 12 motifs 4½" x 4½"
For each color set, you'll need enough scraps
of different fabrics to equal these amounts:

      Orange scraps – ⅛ yard
      Green scraps – ¼ yard
      Yellow scraps – ⅓ yard
      Blue scraps – ½ yard
      Red scraps – ⅓ yard
      Aqua scraps – ¼ yard
      Purple scraps – ⅛ yard
      Border fabrics: 1¼ yards blue,
        ¼ yard yellow, ¼ yard red
Backing: 1½ yards
Batting: 48" by 58"
Binding: ⅓ yard (We pieced ours with scraps.)

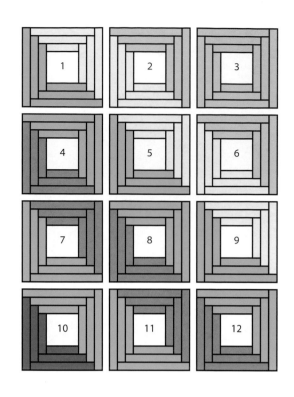

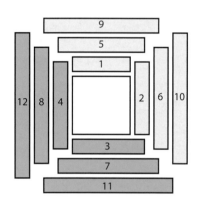

Color 1		Color 2	
Strip #	Length	Strip#	Length
1	4½"	3	5½"
2	5½"	4	6½"
5	6½"	7	7½"
6	7½"	8	8½"
9	8½"	11	9½"
10	9½"	12	10½"

Block Construction

Fussy-cut 12 focus fabric squares 4½" x 4½" for the center of the Log Cabin blocks.

Determine the layout of your center squares. Number each square and note which 2 colors will be used in each block. For example, for squares 1, 5, and 9, color 1 = yellow, color 2 = blue; for squares 2 and 6, color 1 = green, color 2 = yellow.

For each block, cut 12 strips as shown in the chart on the left, noting the color for each numbered log. All strips are 1½" wide.

We like to chain piece the strips on by color groups. Sort and stack the "logs" by color and length.

Sew strip #1 to the top of the focus fabric square as shown, then continue adding strips in a clockwise direction until all 12 strips are on. Finger press the seams away from the center block after each step and gently press with an iron when the blocks are complete.

Join the completed blocks in rows, pressing the seams in each row in opposite directions. Nest the seams, stitch the rows together, and carefully press all the seams flat.

Inner Border

Measure the quilt top length (for the side borders) and width (for the top and bottom borders), which should be about 40½" and 30½". Cut 2 inner border strips 1½" by each of your measurements.

Sew the 2 side borders on, matching the ends and centers. Press the seam allowances toward the borders.

Cut 4 corner squares 1½" x 1½" and sew 1 corner square to each end of the top and bottom borders. Press the seam allowances toward the border strip. Sew the borders to the quilt, matching the side seams, ends, and centers. Press the seam allowances toward the borders.

Outer Border

Measure the quilt top length and width, which should be about 42½" and 32½". Cut 2 outer border strips 4½" by each of your measurements. Cut four 4½" x 4½" corner squares. Add to the quilt as before.

Top Finished!!!

We left our finished quilt top pinned to our design wall for a few days just because it is so fun and energizing to look at. This was a neat quilt for curlycues and hearts quilting. We also quilted in Braxton's name and birth date. ENJOY!

Cuddly Snuggly Quilts ☺ Linda K. Johnson & Jane K. Wells

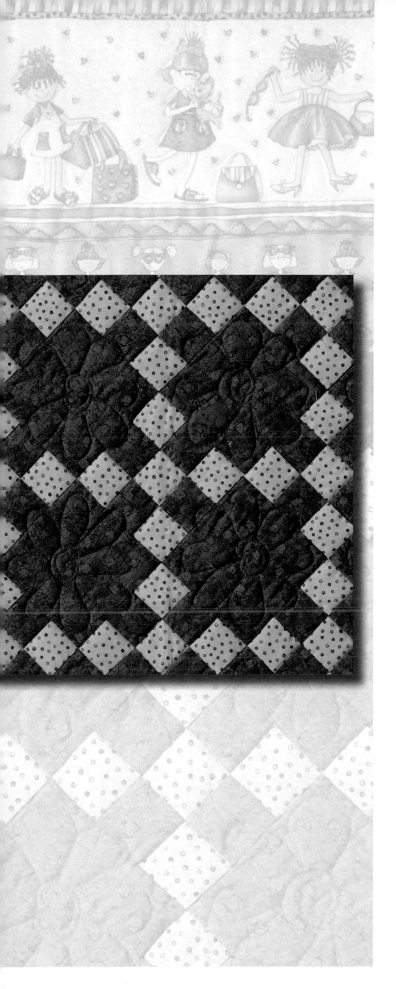

Girls on the Block

52" x 52", designed, made, and quilted by Linda K. Johnson

The girly kids border fabric was the inspiration for the colors of this quilt. Change the personality of the quilt by choosing a different focus fabric. This would be equally wonderful if made with homespun plaids, batiks for a more contemporary look, or solids for an Amish-style quilt. Obtain a scrappy feel by replacing the yellow squares with many different colors. Get as creative as you want, and have fun!

Fabric Requirements

Pink: ½ yard
Blue: ¾ yard
Yellow: ¾ yard
Border print: 1 yard
Backing: 3½ yards
Batting: 60" x 60"
Binding: ⅓ yard for single-fold

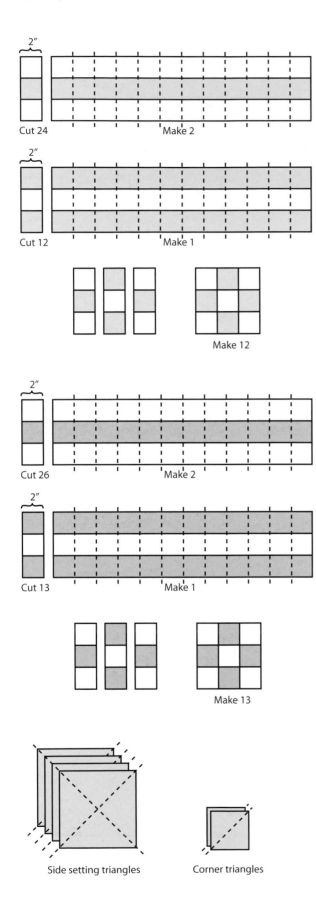

2"
Cut 24   Make 2

2"
Cut 12   Make 1

Make 12

2"
Cut 26   Make 2

2"
Cut 13   Make 1

Make 13

Side setting triangles   Corner triangles

Cutting

Cut 12 squares 5" x 5" from the pink. Set aside the rest for the strip-sets.

From the blue, cut 4 squares 5" x 5", 4 squares 8" x 8", and 2 squares 4½" x 4½". Set aside the rest for the strip-sets.

Nine-Patch Blocks

Cut 5 strips 2" x 24½" from the yellow fabric.
Cut 4 strips 2" x 24½" from the blue fabric.
Make 3 strip-sets as shown. Press the seams toward the darker fabric.

Cut the strip-sets into 2" segments as shown.

Sew 3 segments together as shown, nesting the seam allowances, to form 12 Nine-Patch blocks.

Cut 5 strips 2" x 26½" from the yellow fabric.
Cut 4 strips 2" x 26½" from the pink fabric.
Make 3 strip-sets. Press the seams toward the darker fabric.

Cut strip-sets into 2" segments as shown.

Sew 3 segments together as shown, nesting the seam allowances, to form 13 Nine-Patch blocks.

Assembling the Quilt

Cut the 4 blue 8" x 8" squares twice on the diagonal as shown to make 16 side setting triangles.

Cut the 2 blue 4½" x 4½" squares once on the diagonal to make 4 corner triangles for the opposite corner.

Sew 2 side setting triangles to a Nine-Patch block as shown. Press the seam allowances away from the block. Trim the triangle tips even as shown. Add a corner triangle. Press the seam allowance away from the block. Repeat for the opposite corner.

Arrange the Nine-Patch blocks, alternate squares, and triangles as shown.

Join in diagonal rows. Press the seam allowances away from the Nine-Patch blocks. Join the rows together, nesting the seam allowances.

Square up the quilt top by placing a large square ruler in one corner and trimming the setting triangles a generous ¼" away from the Nine-Patch corners, keeping a 90-degree angle in all 4 corners. Continue trimming in this manner on all sides and corners.

Border

Measure the quilt top length (for the side borders) and width (for the top and bottom borders). Let the design of your focus fabric print determine the width of your borders. (We cut ours 9" wide.)

Cut your borders as determined by the quilt measurements and your chosen width.

Cut 4 corner squares the width of your borders. These could be from another coordinating fabric or pieced from leftover Nine-Patch fabrics. For ours, we cut a 2½" yellow center square and surrounded it with 2½" wide pink strips. We then cut 2 blue 5" squares in half on the diagonal to make 4 triangles and sewed one to each side. We squared up our blocks to measure 9" x 9".

Sew the 2 side borders on, matching the ends and centers. Press the seam allowances toward the borders.

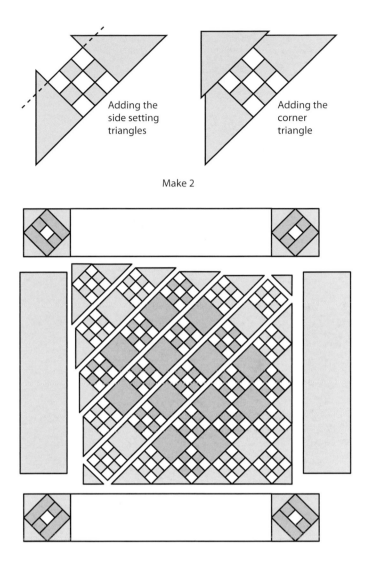

Adding the side setting triangles

Adding the corner triangle

Make 2

Sew 1 corner square to each end of the top and bottom borders. Press the seam allowances toward the border strip. Sew the borders to the quilt, matching the side seams, ends, and centers. Press the seam allowances toward the borders.

This quilt is backed in flannel for a cuddle quilt, but we have also made it in solids as an Amish-style wallhanging and increased the border size to accommodate large Amish-style feather quilting.

Cuddly Snuggly Quilts ☺ Linda K. Johnson & Jane K. Wells

Fit to Be Tied

45" x 63", made by Jane K. Wells for the Basher Children's Home

This is a wonderful quilt that ANYBODY can make. Jane's church, Covenant United Methodist in Fort Wayne, Indiana, has been making variations of this quilt for a children's home for years and even non-quilters help make these gifts of love for at-risk kids.

This quilt consists of 18 squares of novelty fabric and 17 Four-Patch blocks, 9" x 9" finished.

Jane's granddaughter, nine-year-old Madison, is working on her version of FIT TO BE TIED.

Fabric Requirements

Four-Patch blocks:
    ¾ yard each of 2 contrasting colors
Novelty print:
    1½ yards that go well with first two fabrics
Backing: 2¾ yards
Batting: 2 yards of 45½" (poly if you're tying the quilt or cotton/poly if quilting it)

Additional Supplies
Crochet cotton yarn in a coordinating color for tying

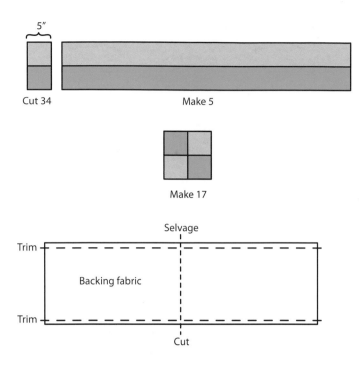

5"

Cut 34   Make 5

Make 17

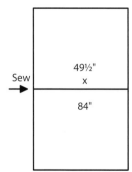

Selvage

Trim

Backing fabric

Trim

Cut

Sew →   49½"
x

84"

Quilt Top Construction

Place the 2 contrasting fabrics right sides together and cut 5 pairs of strips 5" across the width of the fabric (at least 40").

Make 5 strip-sets. Press the seam allowances toward the darker fabric. Cut 34 segments 5" wide.

Flip 1 segment over and pair with a second segment, nesting the seam allowances. Sew the segments together and press the seam allowances to one side.

Cut 18 squares of novelty fabric 9½" x 9½".

Arrange the blocks in 7 rows of 5 blocks each, alternating the Four-Patch blocks and novelty fabric squares. Sew the blocks into rows. Press the seam allowances in alternate rows in opposite directions. Sew the rows together, nesting the seam allowances, and press all the seams in the same direction.

Preparing the Backing

Cut the backing in half across the width, as shown by the dotted line. Trim off the selvages and stitch together along the trimmed edges, right sides together. Press the seam allowances to one side.

The No-Binding Finish

Trim the backing and batting to the same size as the quilt top.

Lay the batting on the floor or large table. Lay the pressed backing on the batting, right-side up. Lay the pressed quilt top on the backing, right-side down. Pin the edges together on all 4 sides.

Sew through all the layers around the quilt with an ample ¼" seam. Leave an 8" opening.

Turn the quilt top right-side out through the opening. Press the edges.

Slipstitch the opening closed.

Use crochet cotton yarn to tie all layers of the quilt together every 4½".

Congratulations on the completion of this simply lovely quilt!

Single Bed Quilt (69" x 91") Variation

Fabric Requirements

Novelty fabric: 2½ yards
2 contrasting fabrics: 1¾ yards each
Backing: 5½ yards
Twin-size batting

The single-size bed quilt is constructed exactly like the cuddle quilt.

Make 8 strip-sets, cut 62 segments 5" wide, and make 31 Four-Patch blocks.

Cut 32 squares 9½" x 9½" for the alternate novelty print blocks.

Arrange the Four-Patch blocks and squares in 9 rows of 7 blocks each. Sew the blocks into rows, then sew the rows together.

Add a simple border. We cut our side borders 3½" wide and the top and bottom borders 5½" wide.

Bouncer thinks this twin-size version of FIT TO BE TIED is also fit for a king!

"Basher Quilts" made by Covenant United Methodist Church in Fort Wayne, Indiana, for at-risk kids at a children's home

Cuddly Snuggly Quilts ☺ Linda K. Johnson & Jane K. Wells

Where's Elmo

40" x 56", made and quilted by Linda K. Johnson for her granddaughter Jordan

This quick and easy quilt was inspired by the colorful motif fabric used in the center squares. This would delight an older child with center squares featuring a theme of their interest. Holiday themes or beautiful batiks would look great here, too.

Fabric Requirements

A minimum of 4 light fat quarters and 4 dark fat quarters.

> To get the scrappy look in our quilt, we used 10 light and 10 dark fat quarters, with lots leftover for future quilts or backing.

Motif fabric: 1 yard, or enough to get 35 center
    4½" x 4½" square motifs
Binding: ⅓ yard
Backing: 2⅞ yards
Batting: 48" x 64"

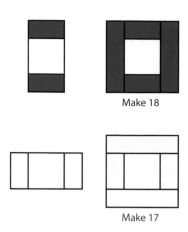

Make 18

Make 17

Making the Blocks

Fussy-cut 35 center squares 4½" x 4½", centering the motifs.

Note: Press all the seam allowances away from the center square throughout the construction of this block.

Cut 2 strips 2½" x 4½" from a dark fabric and sew to top and bottom of a center square. Cut 2 strips 2½" x 8½" from the same fabric and sew to the sides. Make 18.

Repeat the process using the lighter fabrics, sewing strips to the sides first, then to the top and bottom. Make 17 blocks with light fabric borders.

Assembling the Quilt

Arrange your blocks on a design wall in 7 rows of 5 blocks each, alternating the darker and lighter blocks until you are happy with the flow of color and motifs.

Sew the blocks together, pressing the seams in opposite directions on alternate rows. Sew the rows together, matching the seams and nesting the seam allowances.

Finishing

Layer the quilt top with batting and backing. We used flannel on the back to make it very cuddly. Quilt around the motifs and in the ditch, or with any allover pattern.

Bind with straight of grain single-fold binding.

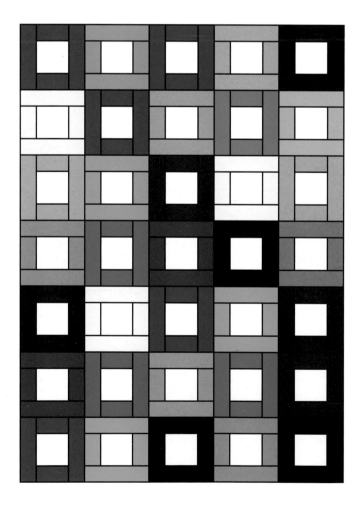

Photo Block Variation

A quilt with photos of a child's school years would make a great graduation present.

The photo blocks are constructed in the same way with one possible exception. If the photo is a little larger or smaller than a 4½" square, or if it is rectangular, you need to adjust the border strip sizes. For example, if you have a photo that measures 4½" x 3½", the side strips will be 2½" wide as before, but the top and bottom strips should be 3½" wide.

Another variation is to use 2 rounds of narrow strips on each block.

WHERE'S MACKENZIE?, 40" x 40", was designed and made by Linda K. Johnson for her granddaughter Mackenzie

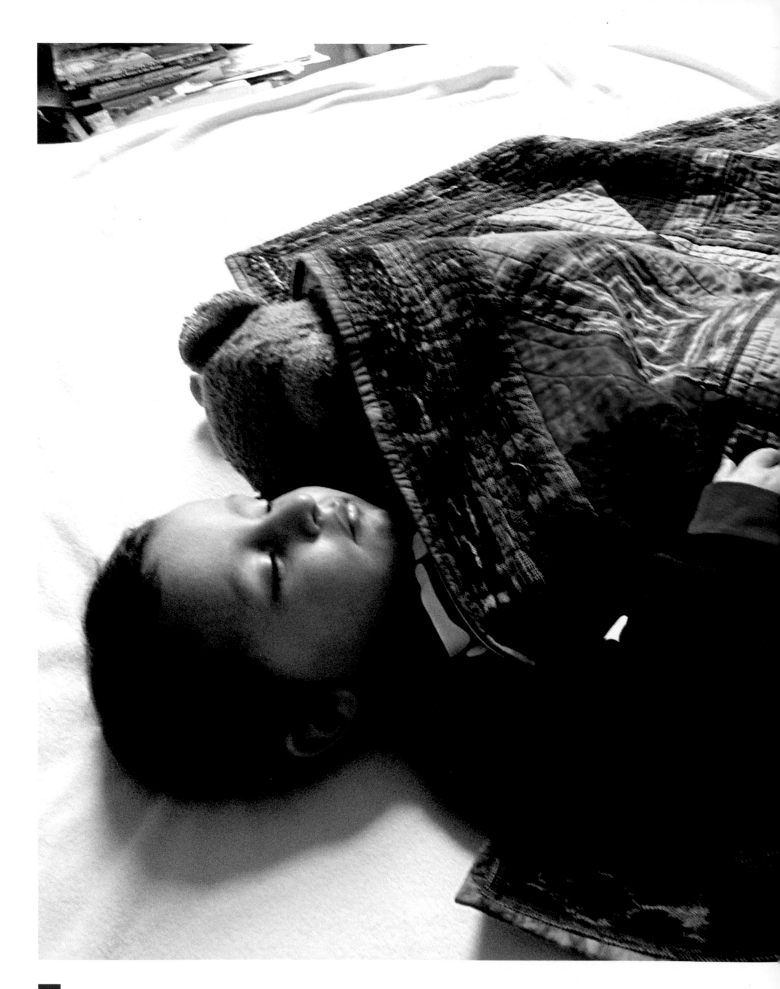

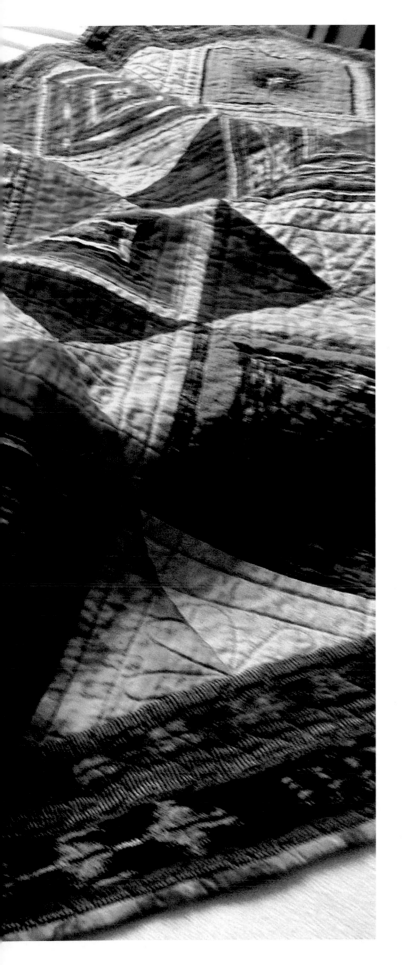

God Bless Landon

38½" x 48½", designed, made, and quilted by Jane K. Wells for her grandson Landon

This is a perfect size for a crib or toddler quilt. It consists of 12 Square-in-a-Square blocks. The center mitered squares, which are made from Guatemalan striped fabric, look like the "God's eyes" we used to weave around sticks as kids. The surrounding squares are made from rich shades of polished cotton.

Fabric Requirements

12 different stripes for the center mitered squares: ¼ yard each
6–8 different plain fabrics to surround the center squares: ¼ yard each
Striped border: 1½ yards
Backing: 2¾ yards
Batting: 46" x 56"
Binding: ¾ yard

Landon is sleeping, God is watching.

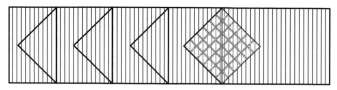

Cutting when stripes are parallel to the selvage

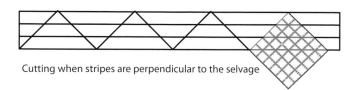

Cutting when stripes are perpendicular to the selvage

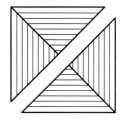 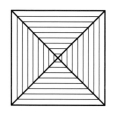

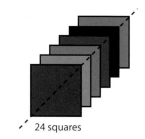

24 squares

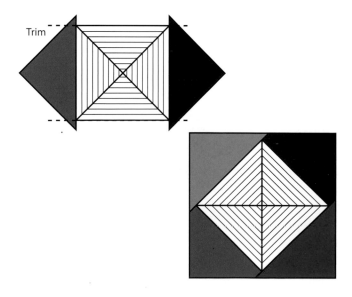

Trim

God's Eye Mitered Squares

Spray starch and gently press the striped fabric, keeping the stripes running in a straight line.

If the stripes run parallel to the selvage, cut strips 8½" wide across the width of the fabric.

Align the diagonal of a 6" x 6" ruler with a specific stripe (base of the triangle) and cut along 2 sides of the ruler, then cut the base to form a 90-degree triangle with two 6" sides and an 8½" base. Repeat, cutting 3 more identical triangles by lining up the diagonal line of the ruler along the same stripe each time. Each triangle has 2 bias edges that need to be handled gently to avoid stretching out of shape.

If the stripes run perpendicular to the selvage, cut strips 4¼" wide and align the diagonal of the ruler with the edge of the strip, then cut 4 triangles as shown in the second cutting diagram.

Arrange the triangles in a square as shown. Stitch together pairs of 2 adjacent triangles, right sides together, matching the stripes. Press the seams in opposite directions. Join the triangle pairs, matching the stripes. Press the seam open.

Trim the mitered square to measure 7½" x 7½". Make 12.

Completing the Blocks

From 6–8 different fabrics, cut 24 squares 6" x 6". Cut each 6" square in half diagonally.

Center and sew 2 mismatched triangles on opposite sides of a God's Eye block. Press the seams away from the center. Trim the tips as shown. Center and sew triangles to the 2 remaining sides. Trim to measure 10½" x 10½". Repeat to make 12 blocks.

Arrange your blocks in 4 rows of 3 blocks each.

Sew the rows together, pressing the seams in opposite directions on alternate rows. Sew the rows together, matching the seams and nesting the seam allowances.

Adding the Border

We often use different stripes on each side of the quilt, but this time we used one fabric on all sides. Either works well.

The border strip was cut 4½" wide. Measure the width and length of the quilt top (should be 40½" x 30½"). Because the corners of the border are mitered, add 10" to both these measurements.

To miter the corner, fold the top border strip back under itself at a 45-degree angle, matching the stripes with masking tape. Pin in place and press. Unpin and hold in place with masking tape. Fold the unit at a 45-degree angle right sides together, lining up the adjacent border edges, and sew along the pressed crease. Trim to a ¼" seam allowance and press the seam open after removing the tape.

Make a backing at least 44" x 54", layer the same size batting and the quilt top. Baste the layers, quilt the quilt, square the sandwich, and bind.

We've actually had people say this was a beautiful art quilt, and Landon's mother asked if we'd put a hanging sleeve on it so she could hang it on his wall when he outgrows it. We chose Guatemalan fabric because we think it is so rich and beautiful and because Landon's mother is from Guatemala. However, our alternate color sample uses other colorful stripes and polka dots in place of the solids.

We made a pair of these for Lev and Maggie, our new twin nephew and niece. What a fun, quick treasure for any child!

All You Can Eat

57" x 57", designed, made, and quilted by Linda K. Johnson

This very happy quilt is super simple, with raw-edge appliqué sewn on during the quilting process. Keep it as a cuddle quilt, or add a hanging sleeve on the back to make it a wallhanging. These fun appliqués in bright primary colors will delight a small child, but you could also change it up with more realistic looking fish and grown-up batik borders for an older child.

Fabric Requirements

Helpful hint: Choose your border fabrics first and pick appliqué fabrics to coordinate with the borders. You could change the color scheme to coordinate with a child's room.

Background: 1¼ yards. A subtle print or batiks that look like water work well. We used a blue sea print on a blue background.

Borders: ½ yard for the sky
    ½ yard of fish fabric for the right side border
    1 yard for the bottom and left side borders

Appliqué fabrics: (Fabrics can be interchanged and used as accents on another appliqué.)

shark: ¼ yard for body plus scrap for contrast top, white scrap for teeth, pink scrap for mouth (We used fabric with multicolored circles for all the eyes, but you can layer different color circles to make your eyes.)

3 small fish: small scraps of contrasting colors for bodies, fins and tails

frog: ⅛ yard dark green (ours is dotted), ¼ yard medium green for belly and lily pad, brown scrap for fishing pole

goose: ¼ yard white plus gold scraps for bill and feet

turtle: scraps of 2 different greens. (We substituted polka dots for the shell.)

plants: ¼ yard of 2 different greens

sun: ¼ yard of 2 different yellows

sign: scraps of black and white

Backing: 4 yards (We used 2 yards of another fish print for the length, then pieced 2 other fabrics to one side to make it wide enough. This makes an interesting back for a child to look at.)

Batting: 65" x 65"

Additional Supplies

Lite Steam-a-Seam 2® fusible webbing: 2 yards or 2 packages
Non-stick appliqué pressing sheet

Appliqué

Cut the background water fabric to measure 35" x 40".

Starch and press the appliqué fabrics.

Use a copy machine to enlarge the appliqué patterns 200%. Trace the reverse of each pattern onto the back of each copy by holding it up to a light.

Trace the reversed *individual* appliqué pieces on the paper side of your fusible web, leaving a ½" space between each shape. Include parts that tuck under another part as shown by dotted lines. Label the parts as necessary to know which part goes with which fish.

Note: Steam-a-Seam 2 has paper on both sides of the fusible web. One layer of paper is more easily removed than the other. Draw the pieces on the paper side that does *not* easily pull away from the web.

Cut the web shapes apart ¼" beyond the drawn lines. Press each shape onto the wrong side of the starched appliqué fabrics you chose for that piece. Cut the appliqué shapes out on the drawn lines, then remove the paper backing.

Place the patterns right-side up on the ironing board. Place a non-stick appliqué pressing sheet over the patterns and position the appliqué pieces on the pressing sheet, overlapping them as indicated on the pattern. Press with a hot iron to fuse the pieces together.

Let cool, then gently peel off the pressing sheet.

Place the shark appliqué at the lower right edges of the water background and fuse in place. Wait to fuse the other appliqués until after the borders are sewn on.

Borders

Cut a 13" x 40" strip for the right border. If you used a directional print, you'll need to cut strips parallel to the selvage and piece them. We fussy-cut ours so the motifs would line up. Sew to the right side of the water background.

Optional: Fuse a piece of webbing on the back of a fish motif and fuse it over the seam line as we did.

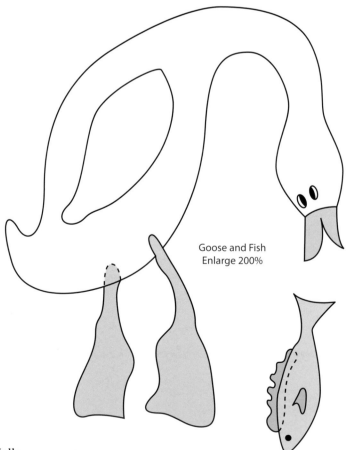

Goose and Fish
Enlarge 200%

All you can eat!

Cut 2 strips 9" wide by the width of the bottom border fabric. Sew them end-to-end, and trim to measure 9" x 47½". Sew to the bottom of the quilt.

Cut 2 strips 9" wide by the width of the sky border fabric. Sew them end-to-end and trim to measure 9" x 47½". Fuse the sun appliqué at the right end of the strip. Sew to the top edge of the quilt.

Cut 2 strips 9" wide by the width of the fabric for the left border. Sew them end-to-end, and trim to measure 9" x 57". Sew to the left side of the quilt top.

Note: If you're using a directional print, you'll need to cut the bottom and left side borders differently— one across the width of the fabric and one along the length of the fabric—so the motifs will flow around the corner.

Arrange all appliqués on the quilt top. Move them around until you are satisfied with their placement, then pin them in place. If you are using a plain water background, feel free to add more plants, fish, and other sea life. You may find fabrics with motifs you want to cut out and fuse on.

Move the background panel with the appliqués to your ironing board. One at a time, remove the pins from an appliqué and fuse it in place.

For the sign, fuse 2 pieces of white fabric together so the background won't show through. Appliqué or embroider the lettering. Position on the quilt and fuse black strips over the edges.

Layer the top with batting and backing and pin baste together.

When machine quilting, edge-stitch each appliqué piece, then echo quilt around each whole motif once. The fishing line is double-stitched with white thread. The worm has a black hook made with quilting thread. The water is quilted with wavy lines and the borders are quilted following the printed motifs.

We loved making this quilt and plan to make it again. Our stash includes many different fish and sea life fabrics that will produce wildly different looks to this pattern.

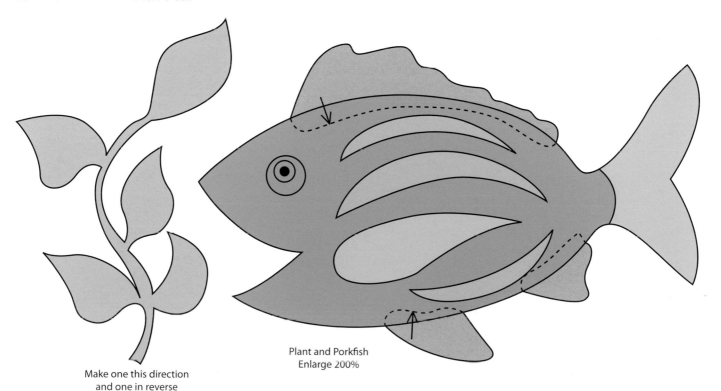

Plant and Porkfish
Enlarge 200%

Make one this direction
and one in reverse

Linda K. Johnson & Jane K. Wells ☺ Cuddly Snuggly Quilts **29**

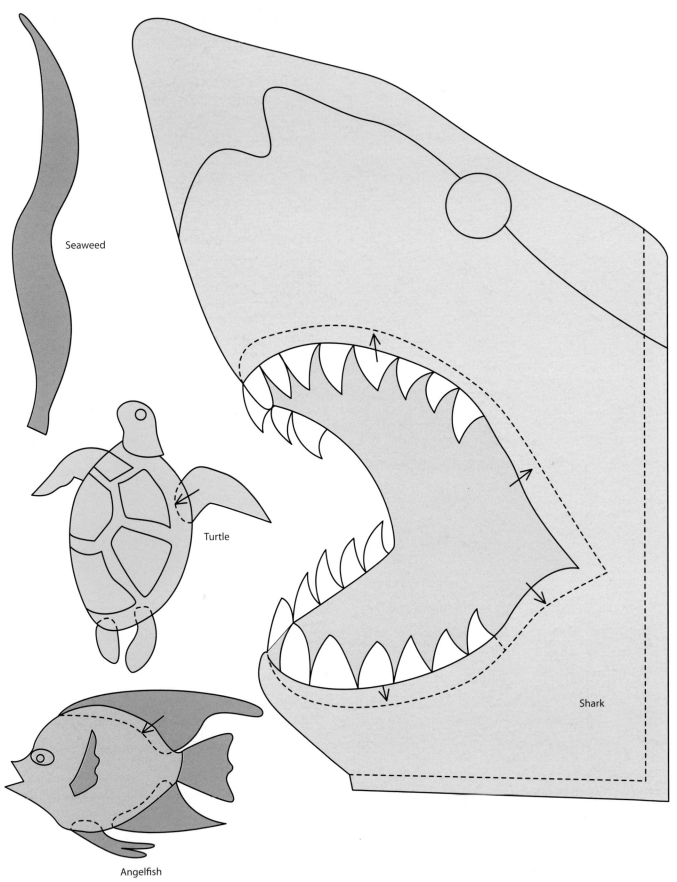

Seaweed

Turtle

Shark

Angelfish

Enlarge 200%

Seaweed:
Make one this direction
and one in reverse

Fishing Pole

Worm

light

dark

Sun

½ of
pattern.
Trace reverse

Frog on Lily Pad

All you
Can eat!

Cuddly Snuggly Quilts ☺ Linda K. Johnson & Jane K. Wells

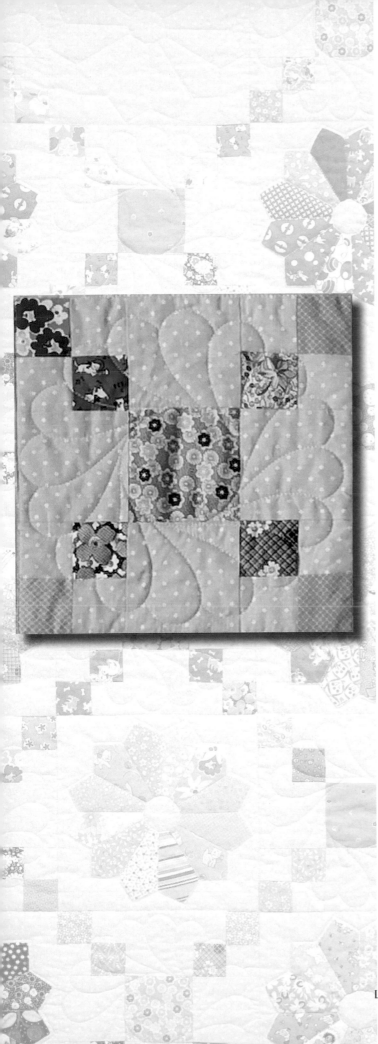

Nine-Patch Pizzazz

69½" x 87½", designed and made by Jane K. Wells, quilted by Paula Reuille, Columbia City, Indiana

We have used both Dresden Plate blocks and focus fabric for the alternate blocks. Instructions and yardage are given for both versions.

Fabric Requirements

Nine-Patch block centers: ⅓ yard
Four-Patch units: 1 yard total (We used a wide variety of scraps.)
Dresden Plates, Flying Geese, and inner borders: minimum of ½ yard of 12 different prints (If you're using focus fabric for the alternate blocks instead of Dresden Plates, 11 fat quarters of different prints will be enough.)
Background fabric:
     5 yards for the Dresden Plate version
     3½ yards plus enough focus fabric to get 17 blocks 9½" x 9½" for the focus fabric version
Flying Geese background (outer border): 1 yard
Backing: 5¼ yards
Binding: ⅓ yard for straight-of-grain, single-fold binding
Batting: 74" x 90" (twin-bed size)

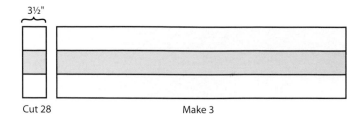

3½"

Cut 28   Make 3

Four-Patch Units and Nine-Patch Blocks

Cut 3 strips 3½" wide from the block-center fabric and cut 6 strips 3½" wide of background fabric.

Make 3 strip-sets as shown. Press the seam allowances toward the background fabric. Cut into 28 segments 3½" wide.

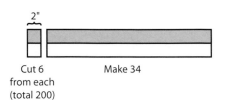

2"

Cut 6
from each
(total 200)   Make 34

To obtain the super scrappy look in the four-patch units, cut strips of 34 different printed fabrics 2" x 13" and cut 34 strips of background fabric 2" x 13".

Make strips-sets with the printed and background fabric strips. Press the seam allowance toward the printed fabric.

Make 100

Cut 6 segments 2" wide from each strip-set. (This will give you 204 segments; you only need 200.)

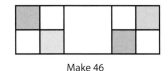

Make 46

Join 2 unmatched segments into four-patch units, nesting the seam allowances. Press the seam to one side.

Cut 5 strips 3½" wide of background fabric into 46 squares 3½" x 3½".

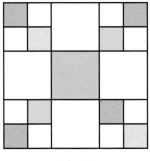

Make 18
Complete blocks

Sew a four-patch unit to opposite sides of the background squares, as shown. Pay attention to the orientation of the four-patch units to establish the X pattern. Press the seam allowance toward the background fabric.

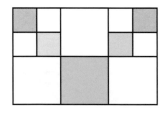

Make 10
Partial blocks

Join the units to make the 18 complete blocks, 10 partial bocks, and 4 corner blocks, again paying attention to the orientation of the four-patch units. The complete blocks should measure 9½" x 9½".

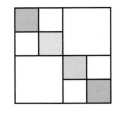

Make 4
Corner blocks

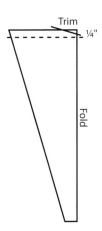

Dresden Plate Alternate Blocks

Cut 17 background squares 9½" x 9½".

Use the template (page 38) to cut out 12 blades from your selected fabrics.

Fold each blade in half lengthwise, right sides together, and stitch across the end with a ¼" seam as shown. Chain stitch all 12 blades at once.

Trim the inside corner seam allowance to ⅛". Finger press the seam open and turn each blade right-side out. Use a rounded tip to push the blade tips out to a sharp point. Press so the blade points are centered.

Arrange the 12 blades in a circle and stitch together along the sides, two by two, until they all form a circular unit. To eliminate threads from showing, start by backstitching ¼" in from the top edge, then stitch forward.

Gently press the side seams open or to one side. If necessary, block the plate with spray starch so that it lies flat.

Clip slightly less than ¼" in at the bottom center of each blade, turn under the seam allowance ¼", and press.

With invisible thread on top and 50-weight cotton thread in the bobbin, appliqué each Dresden Plate to a background square with a blind hemstitch or narrow zigzag. Make 17.

Focus Fabric Alternate Blocks

If you want to use focus fabric alternate blocks instead of the Dresden Plate blocks, fussy-cut 17 squares 9½" x 9½" from your focus fabric. If this is very wasteful or if your focus fabric motif is too small, add background borders Log Cabin-style around the smaller motifs to make a 9½" square. It is easiest to make the blocks a little oversized and then use a 9½" square ruler to cut them to the exact size. (See the focus fabric variations on pages 38 and 39.)

Quilt Assembly

Cut 14 background fabric rectangles 6½" x 9½". Arrange the complete and partial Nine-Patch blocks, background rectangles, Dresden Plate or focus fabric blocks, and the corner blocks as shown. Double-check the orientation of the corner blocks to complete the X pattern.

Sew the blocks into rows. Press the seam allowances in alternate rows in opposite directions. Sew the rows together, nesting the seam allowances, and press all the seams in the same direction.

Inner Border

We made the inner borders with alternating strips of background and Dresden Plate fabrics with a long strip of background fabric in the center of each side.

From the background fabric, cut:
>2 strips 1" x 24" for the top and bottom
>2 strips 1" x 42" for the sides
>8 strips 1" x 6" for spacers

From each of 5 different print fabrics, cut 3–4 strips 1" x 8" (16 total).

Sew 2 color strips alternated with 1 background spacers to each end of both 42" background strips with diagonal seams as shown.

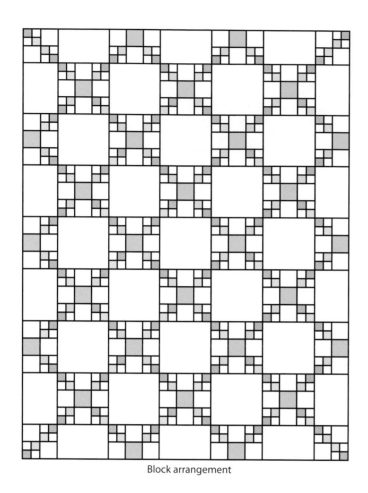

Block arrangement

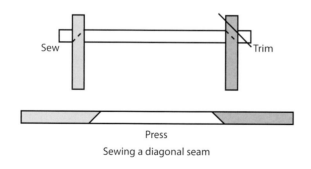

Sew · Trim

Press

Sewing a diagonal seam

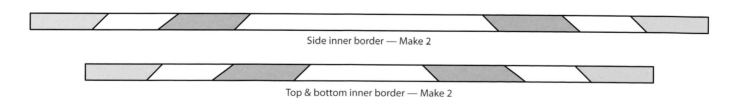

Side inner border — Make 2

Top & bottom inner border — Make 2

Measure the quilt from top to bottom through the center. Mark this length on the two borders, keeping the center of the border at the center of the measurement. Do not trim the excess. You'll need the excess to miter the corners.

Add the borders to the sides of the quilt, starting and stopping ¼" from both ends, aligning the center of the border with the center of the quilt side. Backstitch at the beginning and end of the seam.

Sew 2 print strips alternated with 1 background spacer to each end of both 24" background strips with diagonal seams. Measure across the quilt through the center, mark, and add the borders to the top and bottom as before.

Sew a miter at each corner. Trim the seam allowance and press the seam open.

To miter the corner, fold the top border strip back under itself at a 45-degree angle. Pin in place and press. Fold the unit in half diagonally, right sides together, lining up the adjacent border edges, and sew along the pressed crease. Trim to a ¼" seam allowance and press the seam open.

Outer Border

The outer borders are made with a Square-in-a-Square block flanked by Flying Geese blocks. The outer border is not mitered.

For the Square-in-a-Square blocks, cut 4 squares 4½" x 4½" from 4 different print fabrics.

Cut 8 squares 4¼" x 4¼" from Flying Geese background fabric. Cut each diagonally to make 16 triangles.

Stitch 2 triangles to opposite sides of a center square as shown. Trim the triangles even with the

center square. Stitch 2 triangles to the remaining sides of the square. Trim the block to measure 6½" x 6½". Make 4.

For the Flying Geese, cut 4 rectangles 3½" x 6½" from each of 11 print fabrics (total 44).

Cut 72 squares 3¾" x 3¾" from the Flying Geese background fabric.
Cut 16 squares 3¾" x 3¾" from the quilt background fabric.

Place a background square on the left side of the rectangle, aligning the top and side edges. The square will extend beyond the bottom edge by ¼". Stitch diagonally.

Trim the seam allowance to ¼" and press the background fabric away from the rectangle. Repeat on the opposite side. Trim the tips even with the

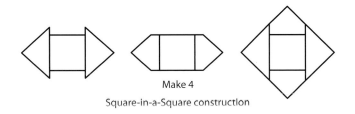

Make 4
Square-in-a-Square construction

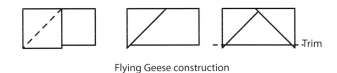

Flying Geese construction

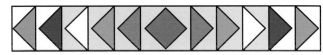

Make 2 side outer border units

Make 2 top & bottom outer border units

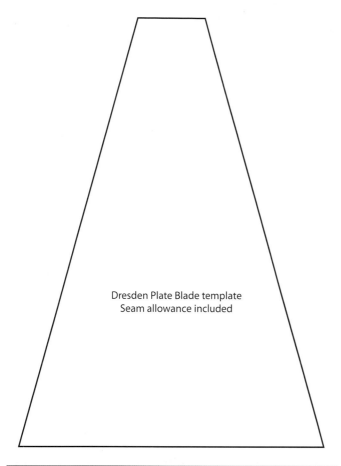

Dresden Plate Blade template
Seam allowance included

bottom of the rectangle as shown to make the geese "float" on the background to complete the Flying Geese block. Make 44.

Sew the Square-in-a-Square and Flying Geese blocks into 4 border units as shown.

Cut 4 strips 6½" x 24½" of background fabric and sew to the ends of the side border units. Measure the quilt from top to bottom through the center. Mark the measurement on the side borders, centering the Square-in-a-Square block. Add to the quilt and trim the excess.

Cut 4 strips 6½" x 17½" of background fabric and sew to the ends of the top and bottom border units. Add to the top and bottom of the quilt centering the square-in-a-square, and then trim the excess.

Finishing

Layer your quilt top with batting and backing and quilt as desired. Ours was machine quilted using a variety of threads and quilting designs. Bind and wrap your grandchild in love! What a fun quilt to cuddle up under. Good night and happy quilting dreams.

Focus fabric version, WILD ABOUT FLOWERS, designed and made by Jane K. Wells

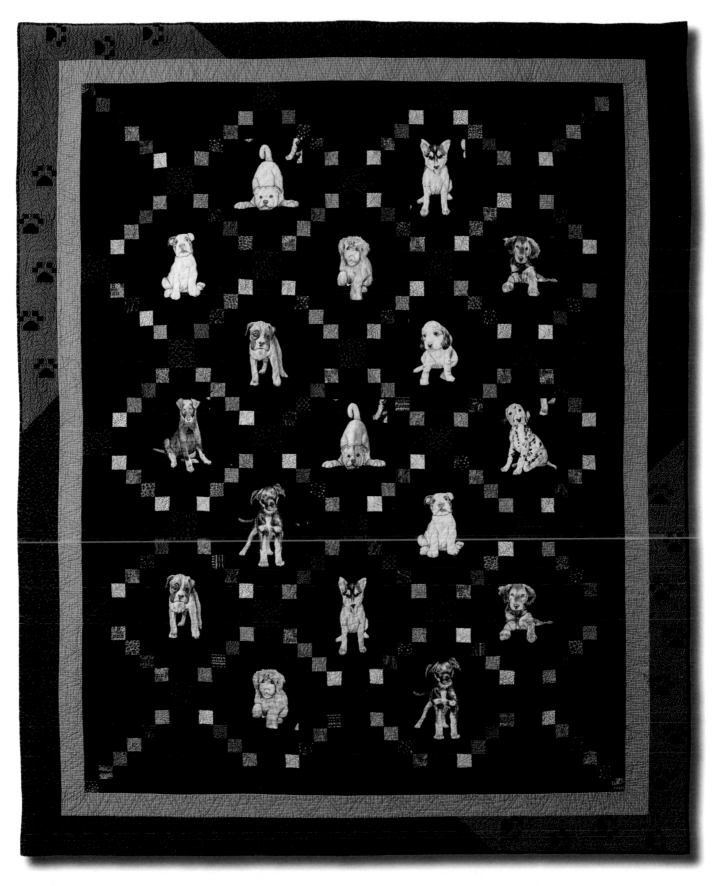

NATHAN'S PUPPY QUILT, 64" x 78", made by Jane K. Wells

Cuddly Snuggly Quilts ☺ Linda K. Johnson & Jane K. Wells

Butterfly Kisses

56" x 72", designed, made, and quilted by Linda K. Johnson for her daughter Jenny

Learn our fun and easy pieced-circle technique. No appliqué here! You may use any theme focus fabric if you choose, but it's not necessary. We chose soft and cozy flannel for both the front and back of this vibrant quilt.

Fabric Requirements

Focus fabric: 1¾ yards or enough yardage to fussy-cut 63 six-inch squares for the block centers. (We used 10 different focus fabric fat quarters and half yard pieces with leftovers.)

Purple: 1¾ yards (or main color of your choice) (We used 4 different purples, ½ yd each.)

7 fat quarters of other colors (We used a variety of lavenders, reds, greens, blues, and yellows.)

Batting: 64" x 80"

Backing: 4⅔ yards

Additional Supplies

Freezer paper

Glue sticks (about 3)

Spray starch

8½" or larger square ruler

5" or smaller round templates (We used a 4¾" CD.)

Open-toe sewing machine foot

Cutting Instructions

Our quilt uses a combination of round, square, and rectangle centers.

Cut 54 squares 9" x 9" for the block backgrounds.
Fussy cut 54 squares 6" x 6" for the round centers.
Fussy cut 9 rectangle or square centers ranging up to 6½" x 6½".
Cut a few 9" x 9" freezer-paper squares. (They're reusable.)

Pieced Circle Blocks

Use your circle template to draw a circle in the middle of a 9" freezer-paper square. Poke a hole in the center with your scissors, then cut out a smooth, even circle on the drawn line. Discard the center circle.

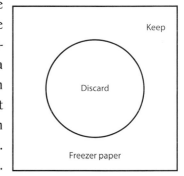

Iron the shiny side of the freezer-paper template to the wrong side of a background fabric square. Draw a pencil or chalk line on the fabric along the cut edge of the freezer-paper circle.

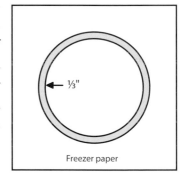

Cut out the center fabric, leaving a ⅓" seam allowance.

Clip the seam allowance *almost* to the freezer paper, about every ½".

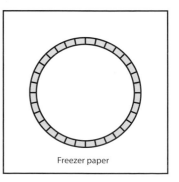

Spray or paint starch the seam allowance from the front so that the

fabric gets wet but not the freezer paper. Working from the back of the block, fold the clipped seam allowance over the freezer paper, pressing one section at a time with the tip of a hot iron. The starch will keep the seam allowance folded back. Check the front of the block to make sure the hole you just created has a smooth even edge.

Working from the back of the block, apply glue stick all around the seam allowance near the fold. Do not get glue on the freezer paper.

Turn the block to the front; position it over a focus fabric square. Press with a hot iron to adhere the background square to the focus fabric. Put the block aside to let it cool while the glue sets.

Repeat this process until you have several blocks ready to be sewn.

Before sewing, gently pull the freezer paper off the back, being careful not to pull the glued focus fabric from the seam allowance.

Lay the block flat on the sewing machine, with the front of the block facing up. Lift one side of the block up, revealing the glued seam allowance and excess focus fabric. You will be able to see the pencil or chalk circle you drew on the ironed fold line.

Use an open-toe foot on your sewing machine so you will be able to clearly see that you are sewing exactly on your drawn line. Stitch all the way around the circle, pivoting with the needle down to get a precise, smooth circle. If you accidentally sew off the line, you can sew again without having to rip out your stitches.

Trim the excess focus fabric to a ¼" seam allowance. Press the block flat. Trim to measure 8½" x 8½". Repeat to make 54 Circle blocks to combine with your Rectangle and Square center blocks.

Rectangle and Square Center Blocks

Cut leftover background fabric into strips to surround the rectangle and square centers.

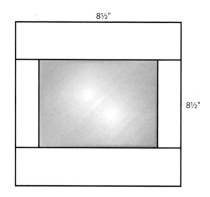

The unfinished blocks should be 8½" x 8½", so the width of the strips will be determined by the size of the center motifs.

For example, if you have a 4½" x 6½" rectangle, it will finish at 4" x 6" when the strips are added. You will need to cut the strips for the top and bottom at least 4¾" wide and the strips for the sides at least 2¾" wide. It is best to cut oversized strips and square up the finished block to size.

Add the strips to your center motifs. Press the seam allowances away from the centers, and square up the block to measure 8½" x 8½".

Continue with various size centers (or all the same size if you prefer) until you have a total of 63 blocks.

Quilt Assembly

Arrange the blocks in 9 rows of 7 blocks each. We placed our main color blocks (purple) on the design wall first, leaving every alternate space blank. When we were happy with the arrangement of the purples, we randomly placed the other blocks in the alternate spaces.

Sew the blocks into rows. Press the seam allowances in alternate rows in opposite directions. Sew the rows together, nesting the seam allowances, and press all the seams in the same direction. We did not add a border to this quilt because we thought it was beautiful as is. However, you may add any border or multiple of borders to make this quilt fit a bed. Layer your quilt top with batting and backing and quilt as desired. We quilted in the ditch and around the circles and rectangles.

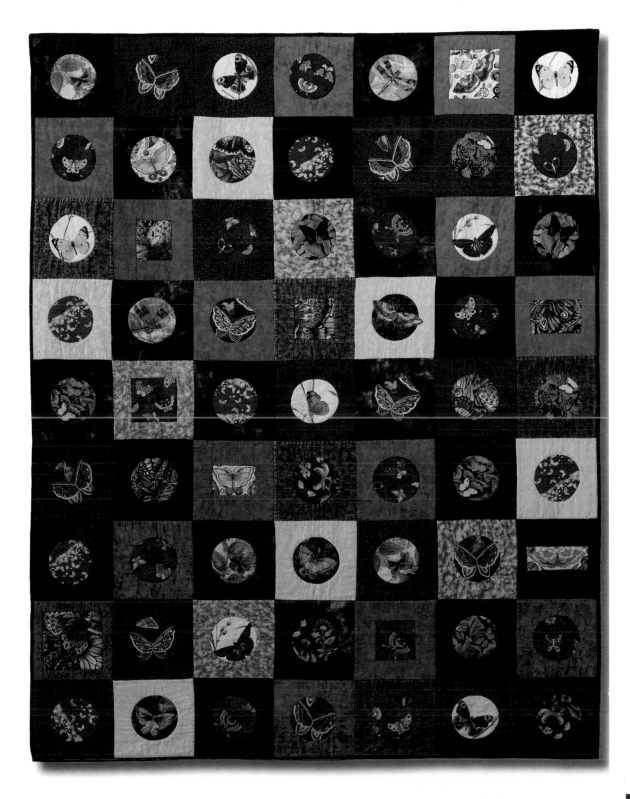

Cuddly Snuggly Quilts ☺ Linda K. Johnson & Jane K. Wells

Woven Wonder

65" x 89", designed, made, and quilted by Jane K. Wells

This quilt offers a great chance to be creative while making a relatively fast and easy quilt. The smaller quilt was "woven" with different Guatemalan fabrics and made as a lap quilt for a teenager. The larger quilt was "woven" with blocks from just one fabric for another teenager's twin bed. We felt it was a little too plain but the broderie perse appliqué from a coordinating fabric transformed it to a lovely art piece.

WOVEN WONDER, GUATEMALAN STYLE
Lap quilt, 42" x 54", designed, made, and quilted by Jane K. Wells

Lap Quilt Fabric Requirements

We used 17 different Guatemalan fabrics and leftovers from our stash. Our plan was to create a few rows using the same stripe throughout the row to support the illusion that the top is actually woven. Other rows are a potpourri of leftover fabrics. A design wall is very helpful for organizing the blocks of this scrappy quilt.

15 different striped fabrics: ¼ yard each
Binding: ¼ yard
Backing: 2 yards
Batting: 50" x 62"

Instructions

Cut 63 squares 6½" x 6½" on the straight of grain from the striped fabrics. Place on a design wall in 9 rows of 7 blocks each, alternating the direction of the stripes to create the woven pattern. We labeled the first square in each row so that we could keep them straight.

Sew the blocks into rows. Press the seam allowances in alternate rows in opposite directions. Sew the rows together, nesting the seam allowances, and press all the seams in the same direction.

Your top is finished and ready for quilting.

We emphasized the woven aspect by free-motion stitching in the direction of the stripes. This is another lovely way to take advantage of the natural appeal of striped fabric.

Twin Quilt with Appliqué Fabric Requirements

Striped fabric: 5 yards
Coordinating flower fabric: 1½ yards (You may need more or less depending on the repeat of the flowers.)
Green: ⅓ yard for flower stems and a few circles
Border, binding, and a few circles: 1½ yards
Backing: 5½ yards
Batting: 73" x 97" or a twin-size batt

Additional Supplies

Fusible webbing such as Lite Steam-a-Seam 2: 2 yards
Round object for circle template (We used a CD.)
Freezer paper
Glue stick
Starch

Twin Piecing Instructions

Cut 140 squares 6½" x 6½" on the straight of grain from the striped fabric. (We cut 6½" strips, then sliced them into 6½" squares.)

Fussy cut 6 squares 6" x 6" from the flower fabric, centering the motifs.

Cut 6 squares 6" x 6" from the green fabric.

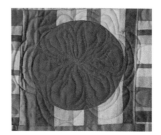

Following the pieced circle directions in BUTTERFLY KISSES (page 41), insert 7 flower circles in 7 striped squares and 6 green circles in 6 striped squares.

Place 14 rows of 10 blocks each on your design wall, arranging the Circle blocks in a pleasing pattern. Sew the blocks into rows. Press the seam allowances in alternate rows in opposite directions. Sew the rows together, nesting the seam allowances, and press all the seams in the same direction.

Broderie Perse Appliqué

Place fusible webbing paper-side up on the wrong side of your floral fabric and use a light box to trace a flower shape. Cut out the fusible webbing ¼" beyond the drawn line.

Cut out the fusible webbing ½" inside the drawn line. This inside piece can be discarded or used on another appliqué. Fuse the ring of webbing to the back of the flower, aligning it with the motif. From the front of the fabric, cut out along the outside edge of the flower. Remove the paper.

Repeat for as many flower motifs as you'd like on your quilt.

Position the flowers on the quilt top in a pleasing arrangement and pin in place.

For the stems, cut bias strips 1 ½" wide. Fold in thirds lengthwise and press.

Position the stems with the flowers, using an iron to encourage them to curve, and pin in place. Use matching thread and edge stitch the stems to the background.

Fuse the flowers in place. Edge stitch to the background or secure them with free-motion quilting.

Borders

Cut 3" wide strips from your border fabric. Measure the length of the quilt down the middle and cut the side borders to this measurement. Add to the quilt top, matching the center and ends. Press the seams toward the border.

Measure the width of the quilt top across the middle, cut the top and bottom borders to this measurement, and stitch on. Press the seams toward the borders.

We quilted with the stripes and emphasized the flowers by quilting on the printed flower patterns. We quilted flower designs on the circles. Have fun!

Cuddly Snuggly Quilts ☺ Linda K. Johnson & Jane K. Wells

Scraps, Inc.

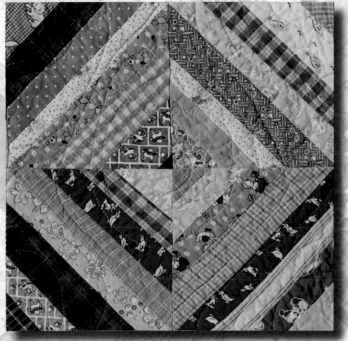

36" x 48", designed, made, and quilted by Linda K. Johnson for her grandson Griffin

This pattern incorporates scraps into a beautiful quilt that is so much fun to make, you may want to cut new scraps! The scraps are pieced onto foundation fabric that stabilizes the bias edges and remains a permanent part of the quilt. Try making this as a large bed quilt, too. The foundation fabric will make it extra warm and cozy.

Fabric Tips

A true scrap quilt will incorporate all different fabrics: plaids, florals, batiks, whatever is left over from any previous quilts, and so on. However, you may also plan your scrap quilt by theme or color, such as a baby quilt, '30s fabrics, homespun plaids, holiday fabrics, etc. You will achieve the best look by including light, medium, and dark values and mixing in large and small prints. Feel free to make larger blocks for big bed quilts.

Fabric Requirements

Lightweight foundation fabric: 1⅝ yards (We used muslin.)
An assortment of MANY light, medium, and dark fabrics, the more the merrier: 4½ yards total
Backing: 1⅔ yards
Batting: 42" x 56"
Binding: ¼ yard

Additional Supplies

6½" square ruler

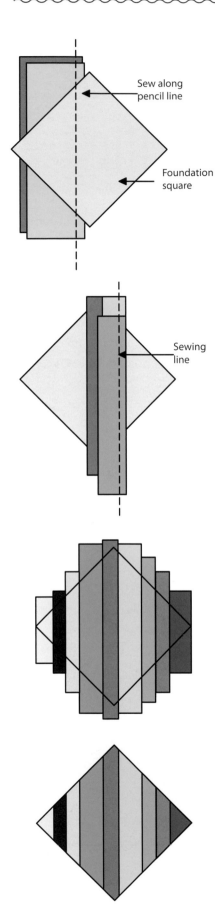

Sew along pencil line

Foundation square

Sewing line

Cutting

Cut 48 squares 6½" x 6½" from your foundation fabric.

Cut scraps (or new fabric) into various width strips: 1", 1½", and 2". The length of the strips does not matter. Each time you add strips to the block, simply select strips long enough to cover the foundation. The excess will be trimmed off after sewing. Triangle-shaped scraps are perfect to use as the last piece at the corners. If you run out of strips that are long enough, piece 2 strips together at a 45-degree angle (see page 36).

Strip-Pieced Blocks

Draw a pencil line diagonally across the foundation squares about ½" away from the center.

Select 2 strips at least 9½" long. Place right sides together and position them underneath the foundation square approximately ¼" beyond the pencil line. Sew exactly on the drawn line.

Open the 2 strips and press.

From now on you will sew with the fabric strips on top. Place a third strip right sides together on one of your first strips, and sew with a ¼" seam. Press open. Continue in this manner until the foundation square is completely covered with strips. Trim on all four sides so your block measures 6½" x 6½".

You can work on several blocks at a time by chain piecing them. If you are using varying widths of strips, make sure you alternate between wide and thin strips. Make 48 blocks.

Quilt Assembly

Arrange the blocks in 8 rows of 6 blocks each, alternating the direction of the strips to form the diamond design. Sew the blocks into rows. Press the seam allowances in alternate rows in opposite directions. Sew the rows together nesting the seam allowances, and press all the seams in the same direction.

This version was planned ahead on graph paper to achieve the colored hearts on the green background. Fun, right? I told you you'd want to make new scraps! Enjoy.

LOVE AFFAIR WITH COLOR, 36½" x 48½", designed, made, and quilted by Jane K. Wells

Block layout

Layer with batting and backing, then quilt as desired.

Make a single-fold binding with 1¼" strips cut on the straight of grain.

Experiment with your blocks to find other pleasing layout designs. These blocks work with an optional plain or appliquéd border.

Alternate layout

Cuddly Snuggly Quilts ☺ Linda K. Johnson & Jane K. Wells

Graduation: Remembering the Good Ol' Days

54" x 66", designed, made, and quilted by Jane K. Wells

When Jane's niece Katie graduated from high school, Jane wanted to gift her with a special memory quilt, knowing Katie is a very special young lady. This is a beautifully graphic quilt consisting of 99 blocks 6" x 6" finished. It is a good example of an easy-to-make pattern that looks like it would be much more difficult to construct than it is.

Fabric Tip

Notice that we used striped fabric in all but two rows, but you could use a few more non-stripes and still get this effect. All the striped fabrics are handwoven 100 percent cotton from Guatemala (sold on our Web site; see page 95). We love the look and feel of this fabric but domestic stripes work fine as well. Guatemalan fabric is 36" wide and domestic is about 40" wide.

Fabric Requirements

Yardage given is for squares to be cut on the bias.

9 different striped fabrics: ⅝ yard each
10 more different striped fabrics: ⅓ yard each
9 photographs printed on fabric: trimmed or
    bordered to measure 6½" x 6½"
Backing: 3⅔ yards
Batting: 62" x 74"
Binding: ⅓ yard for single-fold

Additional Supplies

Very light fusible interfacing: 8 yards
6½" square ruler

Instructions

Assign letters A, C, F, H, J, K, L, N, O, and P to the ⅝ yard fabrics.

Assign letters B, D, E, G, I, M, O, Q, R, and S to the ⅓ yard fabrics.

Fuse interfacing to the back of each striped fabric, then cut the required number of 6½" x 6½" squares from each fabric so that the stripes run diagonally across the squares.

A = 9 blocks	K = 7 blocks
B = 2 blocks	L = 8 blocks
C = 7 blocks	M = 5 blocks
D = 4 blocks	N = 6 blocks
E = 5 blocks	O = 3 blocks (Same fabric as H.)
F = 6 blocks	P = 9 blocks
G = 3 blocks	Q = 1 block (Same fabric as I.)
H = 8 blocks	R = 4 blocks
I = 1 block	S = 2 blocks
J = 9 blocks	

⅓ yard, 36" wide, 1–5 blocks   ⅓ yard, 40" wide, 1–5 blocks

⅝ yard, 36" wide, 6–9 blocks   ⅝ yard, 40" wide, 6–9 blocks

Cutting layouts

Arrange the blocks in 11 rows of 9 blocks each following the layout diagram and using the letter assignments given to the block fabrics. Pay attention to the direction of the stripes in each block. The "P" blocks are the photographs.

When our photos could not be printed at 6½" x 6½", we simply bordered them in black, Log Cabin-style, and then trimmed the photo squares to measure 6½" x 6½".

Sew the blocks into rows. Press the seam allowances in alternate rows in opposite directions. Sew the rows together, nesting the seam allowances, and press all the seams in the same direction.

A	B	C	D	E	F	G	H	I
B	A	D	C	F	E	H	G	J
P	D	A	F	C	H	E	J	G
D	P	F	A	H	C	J	E	L
K	F	P	H	A	J	C	L	E
F	K	H	P	J	A	L	C	N
M	H	K	J	P	L	A	N	C
H	M	J	K	L	P	N	A	R
O	J	M	L	K	N	P	R	A
J	O	L	M	N	K	R	P	S
Q	L	O	N	M	R	K	S	P

Quilt layout

As you can see, after deciding which fabric to put in each place, this is a very simple quilt to construct. We added a couple extra photos on the back for our label and also in the hanging sleeve which reads, "We love you, Katie."

This is a very classy memory quilt for any occasion. Enjoy!

Cuddly Snuggly Quilts ☺ Linda K. Johnson & Jane K. Wells

Rock On!

50" x 62", designed, made, and quilted by Linda K. Johnson

Try a new technique for rocking squares that's easy and fun. This quilt is just the right size for a kid to cuddle in, so you may want to try it in soft flannel. It would also be a great lap quilt for a grandparent, so go bold with batiks or solids. How about a wall hanging made to match your curtains or bedspread? Try a fussy-cut motif for the centers or make more blocks for a bed quilt. Wouldn't this make a great quilt for a college dorm in school colors?

Fabric Requirements

6–12 different color fabrics for the rocking strips and square-in-a-square units: ¼ yard each
Background and border fabric: 1½ yards
Focus fabric for center squares: ½ yard or enough to get twelve 4½" motifs cut on point (optional)
Backing: 3½ yards
Batting: 58" x 70"
Binding: ½ yard

Additional Supplies

4½" square ruler
12½" square ruler

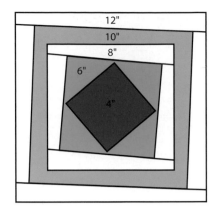

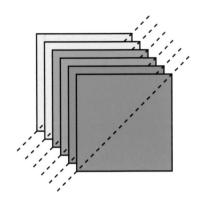

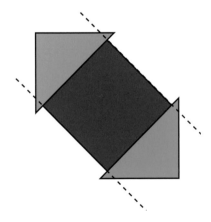

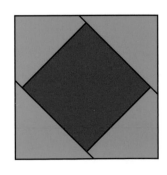

Block Construction

Cut 12 squares 4½" x 4½" for the block centers using each of your rocking strip and square-in-a-square fabrics. If you want to fussy-cut a motif instead, center a 4 ½" square ruler on point over a motif and cut around all 4 sides.

For the triangles to make the 6" square-in-a-square units, cut 12 pairs of 4½" x 4½" squares using each of your square-in-a-square fabrics. Cut each square once on the diagonal as shown.

Sew the resulting triangles to opposite sides of the center squares, matching the centers. Press the seams toward the center, then trim the extending tips even with the square.

Sew 2 matching triangles to the remaining sides, again matching the centers. Press the seams away from the center, then square up to measure 6½" x 6½".

Note: Six of the blocks should "rock" to the right and six to the left. The tilt is established and maintained by the cut of the wedges. Follow the figures carefully.

For the 8" squares, cut 12 rectangles 3½" x 8" from the background/border fabric and cut into wedges— half in one direction and half in the other as shown. The cuts should start and end about an inch from the corners.

Center and sew the bias edge of 2 wedges to opposite sides of the 6½" squares, with the narrow ends opposite each other. Start with the top and bottom wedges for 6 blocks, and start on the sides for the other 6 blocks, as shown. Press the seams toward the center, then trim the wedges even with the square.

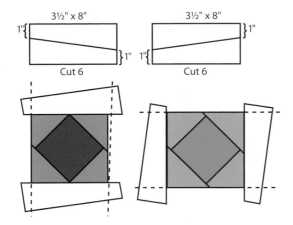

Cut 12 rectangles 3½" x 10" from the background/border fabric. Cut into wedges as before and sew the bias edge to the remaining 2 sides, with the narrow ends opposite each other. Press the seams out, then square up to measure 8½" x 8½".

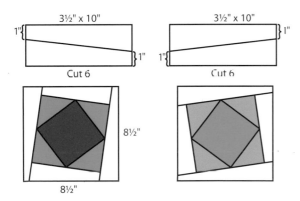

For the 10" squares, cut 12 colored fabric rectangles 3½" x 10" into wedges. This time, the wedges for each block will be cut in the opposite direction from its first set of wedges. Center and sew the bias edges to opposite sides of the 8½" squares. Trim as before.

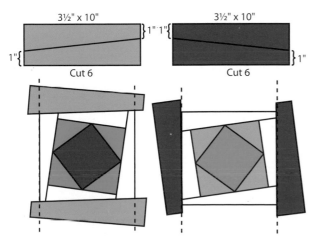

Cut 12 colored fabric rectangles 3½" x 13" into wedges and add to the remaining 2 sides of the squares as before. Press, then square up to measure 10½" x 10½".

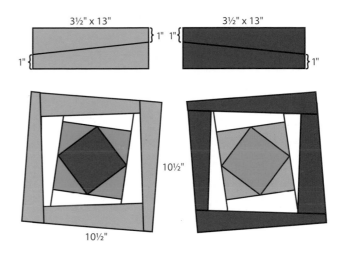

For the 12" squares, cut 12 background/border fabric rectangles 3½" x 13" switching the direction of the cut again. Center and sew the bias edges to opposite sides of the 10½" squares as shown on the next page. Trim as before.

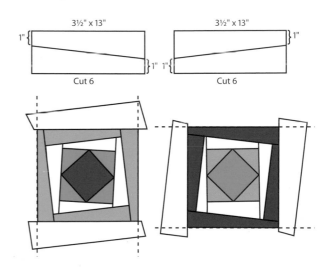

Cut 12 background/border fabric rectangles 3½" x 15" into wedges to add to the remaining 2 sides of the squares as before. Press, then square up to measure 12½" x 12½".

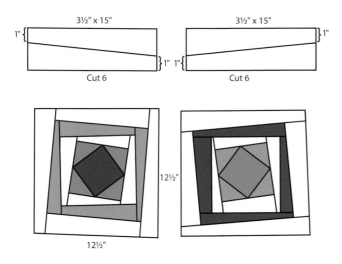

3½" x 15" Cut 6

3½" x 15" Cut 6

12½"

12½"

Finishing

Arrange the blocks in 4 rows of 3 blocks each, with the blocks in each row rocking in the same direction but opposite from the next row (refer to the quilt photo). Sew the blocks into rows. Press the seam allowances in alternate rows in opposite directions. Sew the rows together nesting the seam allowances, and press all the seams in the same direction.

Measure the length of the quilt top through the center. Cut 2 inner border strips 1½" wide by that measurement. Sew a border strip to each side, matching the ends and centers. Press the seam allowance toward the border.

Measure the width through the center, including the 2 inner borders. Cut 2 inner border strips 1½" wide by that measurement. Sew to the top and bottom, matching the ends and centers. Press the seam allowance toward the borders.

Repeat these steps for the outer borders, cutting the strips 6½" wide.

Layer your quilt top with batting and backing, then quilt as desired. Bind, label, and give to your grandchild to cuddle in.

ROCK ON: SOFT AND CUDDLY, 56½" x 70" made and quilted by Jane K. Wells

Cuddly Snuggly Quilts ☺ Linda K. Johnson & Jane K. Wells

What's in Your Cabin?

73" x 89", designed, made, and quilted by Jane K. Wells for her grandson Dakota

Here's a new Log Cabin variation with Roman Stripe alternate blocks and awesome borders. A cool quilt for the older kids—focus fabric suggestions are sports, pets, wild animals, super heroes, princesses, or flowers. What's their interest?

Fabric Requirements

Focus fabric: enough to yield eighteen 3½" center motifs for the Log Cabin blocks

Light, medium, and dark fabrics in small- and medium-scale prints to coordinate with your focus fabric: 3 yards total

Solid fabric: 4 yards for the Roman Stripe blocks, inner and outer borders

Batting: 81" x 97"

Backing 7⅛ yards

Binding: ⅞ yard

Additional Supplies

8½" square ruler

Cutting Instructions

From the focus fabric, fussy-cut 18 squares 3½" x 3½" (for the Log Cabin block centers). It is helpful to use double-sided tape on the back of your ruler so that it doesn't slide.

From each of the print fabrics, cut:
2–3 strips 1¼" and 1½" wide (for the Log Cabin and Roman Stripe blocks)
1–2 strips 2" wide (for the Roman Stripe blocks)

From one of the prints, cut 3 strips 6½" wide for the second border.

From the solid, cut:
6 strips 6½" x 42" (for Roman Stripe blocks and second border)
5 strips 1½" x 42" (for the inner border)
5 strips 2½" x 42" (for the third border)
5 strips 8" wide (for the fourth/outer border)

Log Cabin Blocks

Speed up the construction process by chain piecing; that is, sew the same step on several blocks at once.

Cut 2 segments 3½" long from a 1¼" wide strip. Sew to opposite sides of a center focus fabric square. Press the seam allowances away from the center after each addition throughout constructing this block.

Cut 2 segments from the same fabric 5" long and sew to the remaining sides of the center square.

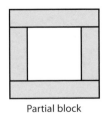

Partial block

Select a different 1¼" wide strip for the second round of logs that contrasts with the first fabric. Cut 2 segments 5" long and sew to opposite sides of the block.

Cut 2 segments 7" long from the same fabric and sew to the remaining sides.

Continue as above for the final round of logs, using the 1½" x 7" and 1½" x 9" segments. Trim the block to measure 8½" x 8½". Make 18.

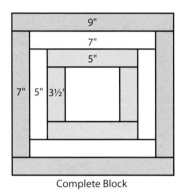

Complete Block

Make 18

Roman Stripe Blocks

Make 4 strip-sets of 5–6 strips 1¼", 1½", and 2" wide by 42" long. Trim to measure 6½" wide.

With right sides together, stitch each strip-set to a 6½" wide strip of solid fabric along both long edges, as shown.

Place the center diagonal line of an 8½" square ruler on the bottom seam line and cut out triangle 1.

Rotate the ruler 180 degrees and place the diagonal line along the top seam line. Cut out triangle 2. You will get 5 triangles from a 40" long strip-set.

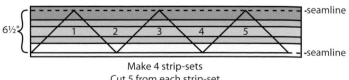

Make 4 strip-sets
Cut 5 from each strip-set

Open the triangles and press the seam allowances toward the solid fabric to complete the Roman Stripe blocks. Make 17. If necessary, square up blocks to measure 8½" x 8½".

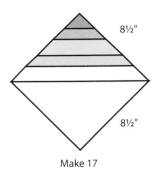

Make 17

Quilt Assembly

Arrange the blocks in an alternating pattern of 7 rows of 5 blocks each, as shown on page 67.

Sew the blocks into rows. Press the seam allowances in alternate rows in opposite directions. Sew the rows together nesting the seam allowances, and press all the seams in the same direction.

Inner Border

This twin-bed size quilt is 40" x 56" before any borders are added. It has a 1" (finished) inner border and a 6" second border, a 2" third border, and a 7½" outer border.

Join the 1½" wide inner border strips, end-to-end as needed. Measure the length of your quilt top down the center. Cut 2 strips to this length and add to the sides of the quilt. Press the seam allowances toward the borders.

Measure the width of the quilt across the center, including the inner borders, and cut 2 strips to this length. Add to the top and bottom. Press as before.

Second Border

Make 2 strip-sets of 5–6 strips of various width fabrics to measure 6½" x 22". Offset the ends of the strips by the width of the strip being added, as shown.

Align the 45-degree angle mark on a rotary ruler with the edge of the strip-set and make a diagonal cut on the left-hand end. Make 2 more parallel cuts 8½" apart, as shown.

Repeat for second set, offsetting the strips and cutting the 45-degree angle in the opposite direction.

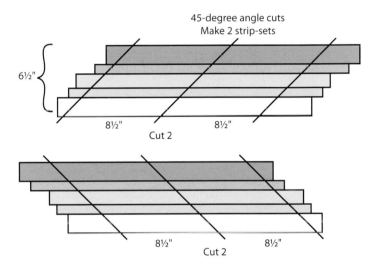

You now have 4 parallelograms to insert in the second border. Position the parallelograms along the 4 sides of the quilt top to continue the stripes established by the Roman Stripe blocks as shown.

Select one of the side parallelograms and cut one end of a solid 6½" wide border strip at a 45-degree angle to match the angle of the parallelogram. Cut one end of a print 6½" wide border strip, again matching the angles. Join both border strips to the parallelogram. Offset the tips ⅜", forming a V-shaped notch ¼" from the ends and sew with a ¼" seam allowance. Press the seam allowances toward the border strips.

Press under a ¼" seam allowance on the quilt-top side of a border strip and place next to the quilt top on your design wall. Use a long ruler to determine the exact spot for attaching this side border so that the border stripes are an extension of the Roman Stripes.

Pin and sew the border to the quilt. Trim the border ends even with the top and bottom of the quilt. Repeat for the opposite side and the top and bottom of the quilt.

Third Border

Measure the length of your quilt top down the center. Cut 2 solid strips 2½" wide to this length and add to the sides of the quilt. Press the seam allowances toward the borders.

Measure the width of the quilt across the center, and cut 2 solid strips 2½" wide to this length. Add to the top and bottom. Press as before.

Outer Border

Make 2 strip-sets 15" x 35" offsetting the strips in opposite directions as shown. Cut 2 parallelograms at a 45-degree angle 11½" intervals from each strip-set (total 4).

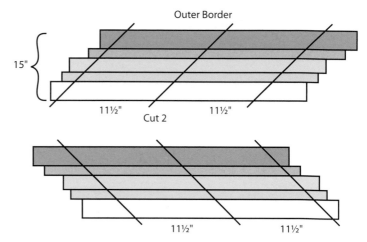

Join with the solid 8" wide border strips in the same way as for the second border.

Add border appliqués as desired.

Make a backing at least 79" x 85", layer the same size batting and the quilt top. Baste the layers, quilt the quilt, square the sandwich, and bind.

Lynne Bogardus of Columbia City, Indiana, chose vibrant butterflies and hummingbirds for her Log Cabin centers and used their bright colors for her Roman Stripe blocks.

Play on Plaids

62" x 79", designed, made, and quilted by Linda K. Johnson

This is a soft and comfy flannel quilt, front and back. Our choice of plaids gives this a traditional look, but wouldn't it be striking in batiks or bright polka dots? Anything goes with this easy-peasy pattern. Ours is a large lap quilt but you can easily make it bigger for a bed.

Fabric Requirements

4 outer border fabrics: ½ yard each

2 or more inner border fabrics: ⅓ yard each

5 half-square triangle fabrics: ½ yard each (shown as row fabrics behind the Scrappy Four-Patch blocks)

7 or more medium and dark fabrics: ⅛ yard each (for the Scrappy Four-Patch blocks)

7 or more light fabrics: ⅛ yard each (for the Scrappy Four-Patch blocks)

Batting: 70" x 87" (or twin size)

Backing: 6⅛ yards

Binding: ½ yard

Helpful hint: Cut your borders, half-square triangles, and setting triangles first, and use the leftover fabrics in your Scrappy Four-Patch blocks.

Additional Supplies

7" or larger square ruler

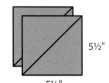

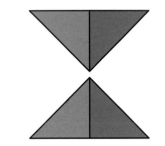

Cut 2 each from the 5 row fabrics (10 total)

Figure 1

Make 2 of each adjacent set (8 total)

Figure 2

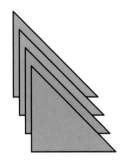

Corner setting triangles
of row 1 and 5 fabrics

Figure 3

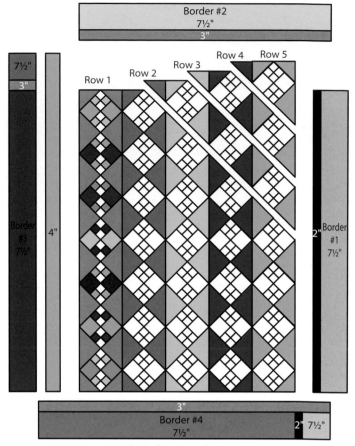

Block placement diagram
Sew blocks together in diagonal rows as shown.

Study the block placement diagram to see how the half-square triangle units create the background for each vertical row of Scrappy Four-Patch blocks. Determine where you want to place your half-square triangle fabrics and then label them with row numbers 1 through 5.

Top and Bottom Setting Triangles

Cut 2 squares 5½" x 5½" from each of the 5 row fabrics as shown in figure 1. Cut once on the diagonal.

Sew 2 sets of adjacent color triangles together as shown in figure 2. Repeat for each color set.

There will be 2 triangles each of row fabrics 1 and 5 left. Save for the corner setting triangles (figure 3).

Side Setting Triangles

Cut a 5" x 35" strip from row fabrics 1 and 5. Place the center diagonal line of a 7" square ruler on the edge of a strip and cut out a triangle as shown in figure 4. (You can mark off a 7" square on a larger ruler.)

Rotate the ruler 180 degrees and place the diagonal line along the top edge. Cut out triangle 2. Cut 6 triangles from both fabrics (12 total).

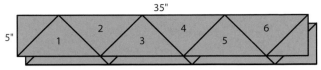

35"

5"

Cut 6 side setting triangles each from row 1 and 5 fabrics

Figure 4

Half-Square Triangle Blocks

Cut 2 strips 7" x 21" from row fabrics 2, 3, and 4. Cut 1 strip 7" x 21" from row fabrics 1 and 5.

Place strips of 2 adjacent colors right sides together. Draw a vertical grid 7" apart, then add diagonal lines, as shown in figure 5. Sew ¼" from both sides of the diagonal lines as indicated by the dotted lines.

Cut on the solid lines to make 6 half-square triangles. Press the seams to one side then trim to measure 6½" x 6½", centering the diagonal seam as shown in figure 6.

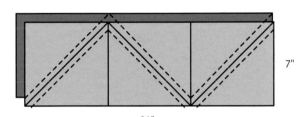

7"

21"

Place right sides together

Figure 5

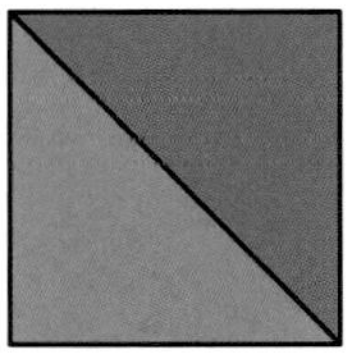

Make 6 of each set
(24 total)
Figure 6

Scrappy Four-Patch Blocks

For each block, cut 2 squares 3½" x 3½" from a medium or dark fabric (figure 6).

Make a strip-set from 2 strips 2" x 8", one dark and one light. Cut into 4 segments 2" wide. Join as shown in figure 8 to form 2 four-patch units.

Join the 3½" squares and four-patch units as shown in figure 9 to complete the block. Repeat these steps to make a total of 35 blocks, always keeping the lightest value in the position shown in white.

3½"

Cut 2

Figure 7

2"

Cut 4   Make 1

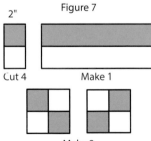

Make 2

Figure 8

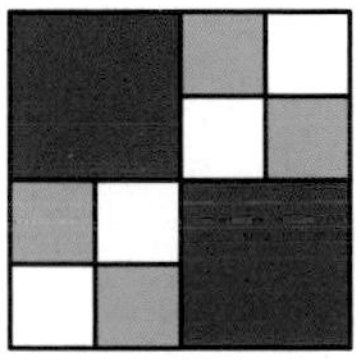

Make 35

Figure 9

Quilt Top Assembly

Arrange the Scrappy Four-Patch blocks, half-square triangle blocks, and setting triangles as shown in the block placement diagram. Sew in diagonal rows, pressing the seam allowances toward the Four-Patch blocks to make it easier to match the row seams later. Trim the extended tips of the setting triangles on each row even with the Scrappy Four-Patch blocks as shown in figure 10.

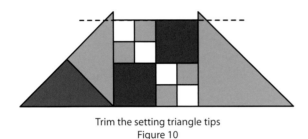

Trim the setting triangle tips
Figure 10

Sew the rows together, matching the seams and nesting the seam allowances. Press. Trim the setting triangles ¼" away from the points of the Scrappy Four-Patch blocks as shown in figure 11.

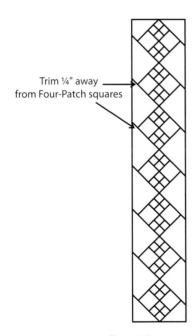

Trim ¼" away from Four-Patch squares

Figure 11

Border Cutting & Assembly

Cut 2 strips 7½" x 40" from each of the 4 border fabrics.

Cut each of the inner borders as follows:
2 strips 2" x 40" (inner border 1)
2 strips 3" x 40" (inner border 2)
2 strips 3" x 40" (inner border 3)
2 strips 4" x 40" (inner border 4)

Join matching pairs of all the border fabric strips end-to-end.

Cut a 7½" x 7½" cornerstone from 2 of the half-square triangle fabrics (total 2).

Cut a 2" x 7½" rectangle from inner border #1 fabric and a 3" x 7½" rectangle from inner border #2 fabric.

Piece border #3, sewing a 7½" x 7½" cornerstone square to a 3" x 7½" rectangle of inner border #2 fabric. Add to the border #3 strip.

Piece border #4, sewing a 7½" x 7½" cornerstone square to a 2" x 7½" rectangle of inner border #1 fabric. Add to the border #4 strip.

Sew all the inner and outer border strips together as shown in the block placement diagram. Measure the length of the quilt down the middle. Cut border 1 this length and sew it to the right side of the quilt. Press all seams toward the inner borders.

Measure the width of the quilt through the middle, including border 1. Cut border 2 to this length and sew to the top of the quilt, matching the ends.

Measure the length of the quilt, including border 2. Cut border 3 to this length, and sew it to the left side of the quilt. Measure the width of the quilt, cut border 4 to this length, and sew to the bottom of the quilt.

We backed this quilt with leftover flannel fabric pieced together for a truly scrappy, soft quilt.

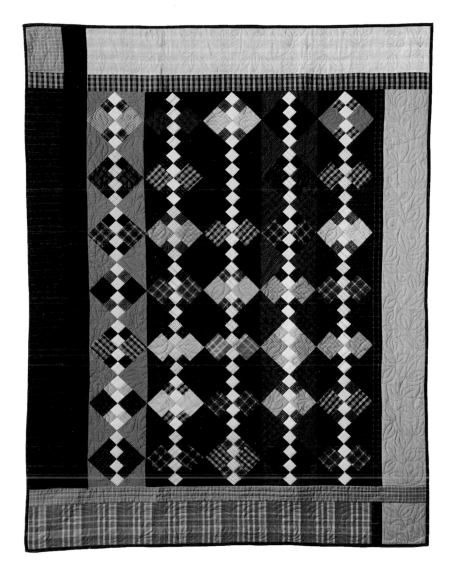

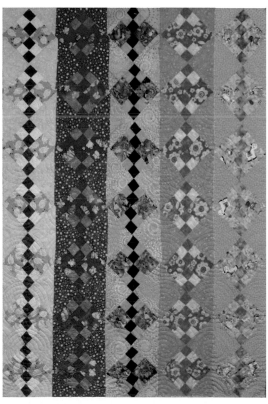

Deb Roehm of Roanoke, Indiana, chose bright and cheery fabrics to make this quilt for her granddaughter.

Cuddly Snuggly Quilts ☺ Linda K. Johnson & Jane K. Wells

Garrett's Crazy Cabins

45" x 63", designed, made, and quilted by Jane K. Wells for her grandson Garrett

This was made as a baby quilt that could also become a comfy nap quilt for a toddler. This same pattern could be made as a single bed size for an older child by adding wider borders or another row of horizontal and vertical blocks. The 11" by 12½" blocks are very simple for a beginner and yet they leave much room for creativity. The 1" sashing with Friendship Star connectors adds pizzazz.

Fabric Requirements

12 different focus fabric motifs ranging in size from 5"–9"

Many coordinating scraps: 2–3 yards total for the surrounding strips, cut into different width strips from 5"–15" long. These strips can be rectangular or wedge-shaped but must have straight sides.

Sashing: ⅔ yard

Border: 1 yard

Backing: 3⅛ yards

Batting: 53" x 71"

Binding: ½ yard

Additional Supplies

Spray starch

13" or larger square ruler

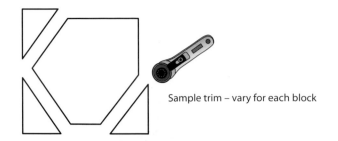

Sample trim – vary for each block

Trimming the surrounding strip

Trimming the completed block—make 12

Crazy Cabin Blocks

Trim a focus fabric motif into a shape with 5 or 6 sides.

Cut a surround strip a couple of inches longer than a side and sew it to that side. Press the seam allowance toward the strip. Use a ruler to trim the ends of the strip even with 2 adjacent sides as shown.

Continue adding and trimming strips in a counterclockwise direction until the block is close to 11½" by 13". At this point, trim the excess and/or add more strips only where needed. We like to heavily spray starch here to help keep the cross-grain edges from stretching out of shape.

Trim the completed block to measure 11½" x 13". Make 12.

After completing one block, we suggest you chain piece 5 or 6 blocks at a time to speed things up a bit. Just don't forget to admire each block as you're piecing it!

Sashing

Cut 9 sashing strips 1½" x 11½".
Cut 8 sashing strips 1½" by 13".
Cut 6 sets of 5 squares 1½" x 1½" (30 total) for the Friendship Star sashing connectors (star points and cornerstones). Each set may be a different color.

To keep organized, place the quilt blocks, sashing strips, and 6 cornerstone 1½" squares on your design wall in 4 rows of 3 blocks each. If you are using different colors for your stars, this is where you will keep track of the star point color placement (see the block placement diagram, page 77).

Place a star point (1½" square) right sides together on the end of all 17 sashing strips, matching the square with the adjacent cornerstone. Sew a diagonal seam as shown (in the same direction on each square). Fold the square back on the stitching line and press toward the outside edge of the sashing strip. Trim the middle section to ¼".

Sew a second 1½" square to the other end of the central sashing strips—3 of the 11½" strips and 4 of the 13" strips—sewing the diagonal seam in the same direction as before, matching the color of the adjacent cornerstones. Press and trim.

Sew the rows of blocks and the 11½" sashing strips together, pressing the seam allowances toward the sashing strips.

Sew the rows of 13" sashing strips and cornerstones together, pressing the seam allowances toward the star points.

Join the rows together, matching the seams and nesting the seam allowances.

Border

Measure the length of the quilt through the middle. Cut two 1½" wide inner border strips to this length from the sashing fabric. Add to the sides. Press the seam allowances toward the border.

Measure the width of the quilt through the middle. Cut two 1½" wide inner border strips to this length and add to the top and bottom of the quilt.

In the same way, cut the outer border strips 4½" wide and add to the quilt.

Admire a job well done!!!

Sew a diagonal seam, press, and trim.

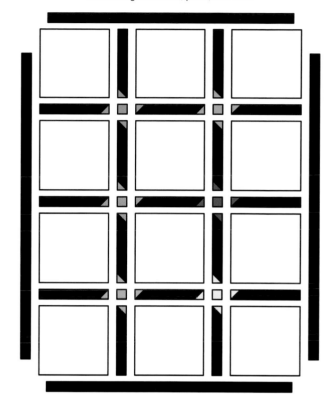

Block placement guide

Georgetta Simmons, Fort Wayne, Indiana, made this version called CRAZY CATS.

Cuddly Snuggly Quilts ☺ Linda K. Johnson & Jane K. Wells

Guatemalan Jewels

88" x 93", designed and made by Linda K. Johnson; machine quilted by Paula Reuille, Columbia City, Indiana

Our blocks are made with handwoven Guatemalan cotton striped fabrics and the sashing is polished cotton, which provides a wonderful contrast to the textured Guatemalan fabrics. This quilt was made as a wedding gift for my daughter, Julia, and her husband, Cody.

Fabric Requirements

7 different striped fabrics: ½ yard each
7 different contrasting fabrics: ¼ yard each of for block border #1
9 different fabrics: ½ yard each for sashing, outer borders, and flower appliqués
Black: ¾ yard for cornerstones and binding
Pink floral: ½ yard for the setting triangles
Green print: ⅓ yard for the vines
Borders: 2½ yards
Batting: 96" x 101" (queen size)
Backing: 6 yards (or 2¾ yards 102" wide fabric)
Additional appliqué fabrics: ½ yard total assorted greens for the leaves and birds; ¼ yard for the yellow flower centers; small scraps red and gold for birds

Additional Supplies

Spray starch
6½" square ruler
Non-stick appliqué pressing sheet

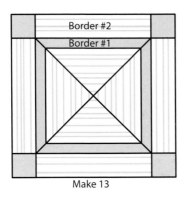

Make 13

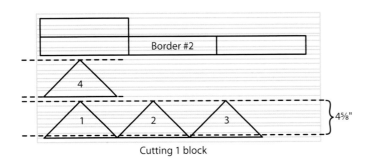

Cutting 1 block

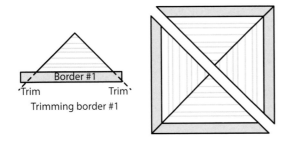

Trimming border #1

Pressing and Cutting

Instructions are for one block.

Spray starch the striped fabric and press with a hot iron, keeping the stripes running in a straight line. The starch will stabilize the fabric and make it easier to work with bias cuts.

Cut one strip 4⅝" wide along a stripe. Place the diagonal line of a 6½" square ruler along the base line stripe and cut on 2 sides of the ruler for the first triangle. Repeat for a total of 4 triangles. If you need to cut a second strip, start on a base line stripe identical to the first as shown in the cutting diagram.

From the same striped fabric, cut four 10" x 1¾" strips for border #2.

Cutting tip: You will have enough triangles for 2 blocks by using the inverted triangles between the first set of triangles. They will have a different base line stripe.

From a contrasting fabric, cut four 11" x 1¼" pieces for border #1. Cut four 1¾" x 1¾" squares for the cornerstones.

Block Construction

Center and sew a border #1 strip to each triangle base, as shown. Press the seam allowances of 2 opposite triangles toward the border; press the remaining 2 seam allowances toward the center. Trim the ends even with the triangle sides.

Sew 2 triangles together, matching the stripes and nesting the seam allowances. Repeat. Press the seam allowances in opposite directions. Stitch together these 2 new triangles, nesting the seam allowances. Press the seam allowance open, using spray starch if necessary. You now have a 10" block.

Sew 2 border #2 strips to opposite sides of the block and press the seam allowances toward the strips.

Sew the 1¾" squares onto each end of the remaining 2 border #2 strips. Press the seam allowances toward the strips. Stitch these 2 borders on, nesting the seams. Press the seam allowances toward the strips. You now have a 12½" block.

Repeat these steps to make 13 blocks.

Quilt Assembly

Arrange the 13 blocks on point on your design wall, leaving 3" between each block.

Cut 4 sashing strips 3" x 12½" from each of 9 different fabrics. Cut 24 black cornerstones 3" x 3". Place the sashing strips and cornerstones on the design wall as shown. Keep rearranging the sashing and blocks until you like the flow of color.

Sew the sashing strips, cornerstones, and blocks into 11 diagonal rows as shown. Press all the seam allowances towards the sashing strips. Join rows 1 and 2; rows 3 and 4; rows 5, 6, and 7; rows 8 and 9; and rows 10 and 11 to make 5 row units.

Cut 2 squares 18" x 18" twice on the diagonal to make 8 side setting triangles. Cut 8 strips 4½" x 26½" from the sashing fabrics. Center and sew a strip to the long side of each of the side setting triangles. Press the seam allowances toward the strip and trim.

Cut 2 squares 6" x 6" once on the diagonal to make 4 corner setting triangles. Cut 2 strips 4½" x 17" from each of 4 different fabrics. Sew 2 matching strips to each triangle. Stop stitching ¼" from the right-angle corner, and then miter the seam. Trim the long side of the triangle to complete the corner setting triangles.

Sew a side setting triangle to each end of 4 diagonal rows and a corner setting triangle to each end of the middle row as shown on page 84. Trim the tips of the triangles as shown.

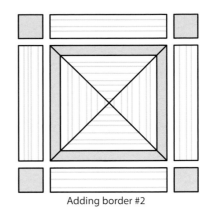

Adding border #2

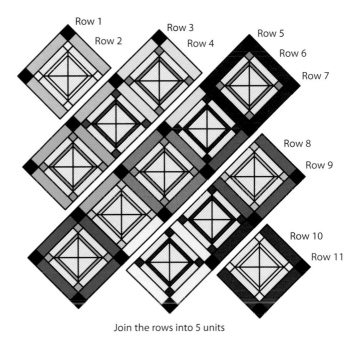

Row 1
Row 2
Row 3
Row 4
Row 5
Row 6
Row 7
Row 8
Row 9
Row 10
Row 11

Join the rows into 5 units

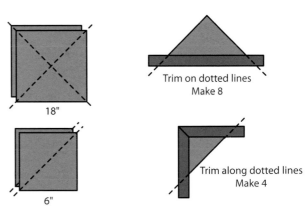

18"

Trim on dotted lines
Make 8

6"

Trim along dotted lines
Make 4

To miter the corner, fold the top border strip back under itself at a 45-degree angle. Pin in place and press. Fold the unit in half diagonally, right sides together, lining up the adjacent border edges, and sew along the pressed crease. Trim to a ¼" seam allowance and press the seam open.

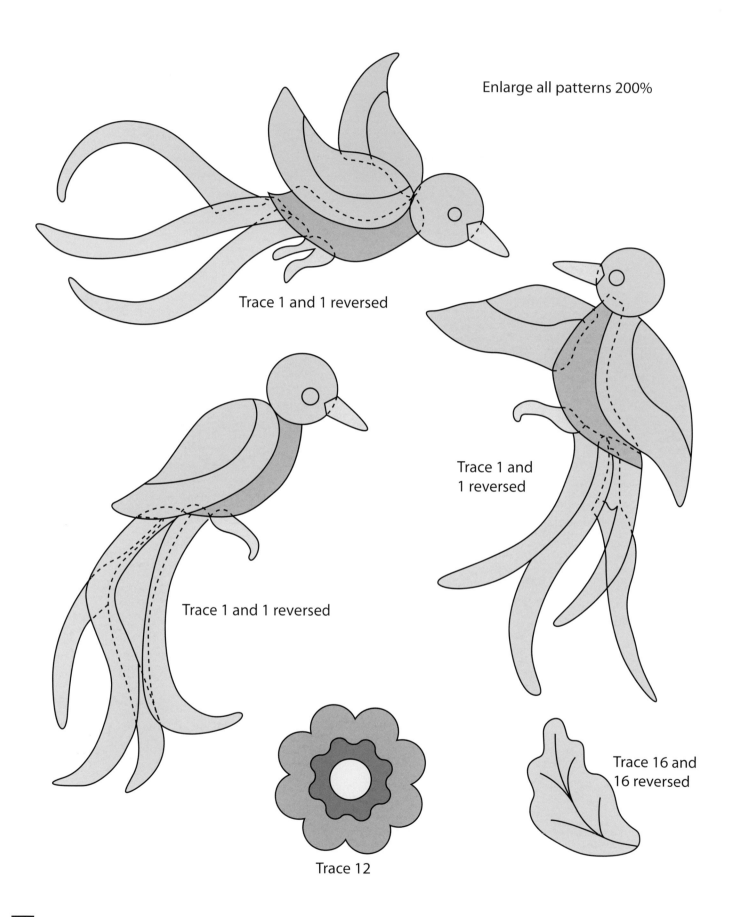

Enlarge all patterns 200%

Trace 1 and 1 reversed

Trace 1 and
1 reversed

Trace 1 and 1 reversed

Trace 16 and
16 reversed

Trace 12

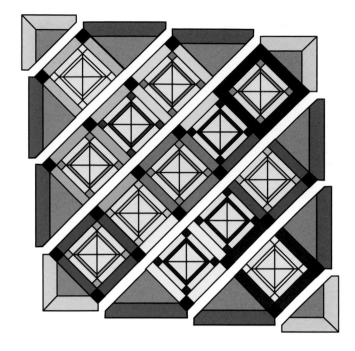

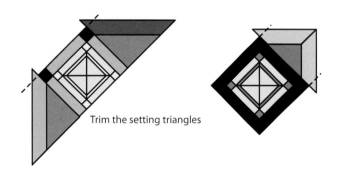

Trim the setting triangles

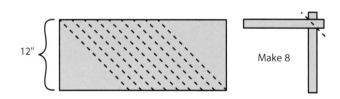

12" {

Make 8

Sew the rows together, nesting the seam allowances. Add the last 2 corner setting triangles.

Note: If you want a lap quilt or wallhanging, you're done. If you want a bed quilt, continue with border directions below.

Outer Borders with Optional Raw-Edge Applique'

Because we made this quilt for a queen size bed, we cut our borders wider for the top and bottom (10") than for the sides (7½"). We added our appliqué after the borders were sewn on, which made the blanket-stitching technique difficult. We recommend you appliqué the borders before you sew them onto the quilt top!

Measure the length of the quilt through the middle (it should be about 69½"). Cut 2 border strips 7½" wide by the length of the quilt plus an inch or so to accommodate possible shrinkage during the appliqué.

Measure the width of the quilt through the middle, add 14½" for the 2 side borders (it should be about 83½"). Cut 2 border strips 10" wide by this measurement plus an inch.

Cut 16 bias strips 1" wide from your vine fabric as shown. Make 8 sections of 2 pieces each, joining them with a 45-degree seam. Sew 2 strips together at a 45-degree angle to make eight 32" vine pieces

Press the vine pieces in thirds lengthwise wrong sides together. Press the vine in a gentle curve on one end of a side border piece, with the vine extending 1" beyond the end of the border. Pin in place and blanket stitch on both sides of the vine, stopping the stitching about 3" away from the end of the border. Repeat with vines on each end of both side borders.

Place the side borders on a design wall. Position the top and bottom borders adjacent to the side borders to determine where to start and stop the vines on the top and bottom border pieces. Repeat the pressing, pinning, and stitching on the top and bottom vines, stopping the stitching about 3" away from the border edges.

Starch and press the appliqué fabrics.

Use a copy machine to enlarge the appliqué patterns 200%. Trace the reverse of each pattern onto the back of these copies by holding them up to a light.

Trace each bird and half the leaves from both sides of the patterns.

Trace the reversed *individual* appliqué shapes (include the parts that tuck under another part as shown by dotted lines) on the paper side of your fusible web, leaving ½" space between each shape. (If you're using Steam-a-Seam 2, it has paper on both sides of the fusible web; write on the paper side that does not easily pull away from the web.) Label the parts as necessary to know which part goes with which bird.

Cut the web shapes apart with about ¼" margin outside of your drawn lines. If using double-paper web, peel the paper off the unmarked side. Press each shape onto the wrong side of the starched appliqué fabric for that piece.

Cut out the appliqué shape on the drawn lines and remove the paper backing.

For each bird and flower, place the pattern copy right-side up on an ironing board. Place a non-stick appliqué pressing sheet on top of the pattern. Position the appliqué shapes on the pressing sheet, overlapping them as indicated on the pattern, and press with a hot iron to fuse the pieces into one unit.

Let it cool, then gently peel off the pressing sheet.

Arrange and pin the appliqué unit to the borders, referring to the quilt photograph for placement. Press with a hot iron to fuse each appliqué in place. Blanket stitch around each appliqué with decorative thread (we used black).

Measure the quilt length through the middle and trim the side borders to this measurement, being careful not to cut off the ends of the vines. Sew the side borders to the quilt top. Press the seam allowances towards the border.

In the same way, measure the quilt width and trim the top and bottom borders. Add to the quilt, making sure the vine ends are not caught in the seam. Press as before.

Arrange the vine ends so they meet in a nice curve, and trim to fit. You do not need to finish the vine ends; they will be covered with appliqué. Finish stitching the vines around the corners, and then place a flower or leaf appliqué over the connection. Blanket-stitch around the appliqué.

To make the quilt bigger, we added another border of leftover sashing fabric strips cut 3" wide and joined with a 45-degree seam. You could use just one fabric instead of piecing all the short pieces.

You are now ready to layer with backing and batting and quilt as desired.

Cuddly Snuggly Quilts ☺ Linda K. Johnson & Jane K. Wells

Frog Frenzy

54" x 67½", designed, made, and quilted by Jane K. Wells

This fun quilt is a perfect bed topper or cuddle quilt, and it's a great stashbuster. It is interesting to make because each block is different. We hope you have as much fun making this as we did. There are many choices and chances to be creative and sometimes, that is what we quilters are all about! Let's begin!

Fabric Requirements

Purple: 1½ yards for sashing and border
Green: 1⅛ yards for sashing and border
12 center motifs: Use one or a variety of novelty fabrics. Nine blocks call for a 4½" x 4½" motif. Larger motifs are used in block 6 (6½"); block 8 (your choice); and block 10 (6"). Center motif squares are positioned in the center of all the blocks.
(We used lots of different fabrics from our stash that coordinated with our novelty, border, and sashing fabrics.)
Backing: 3⅝ yards
Batting: 62" x 75"
Binding: ⅞ yard

The Blocks

Block 1 - Nine-Patch

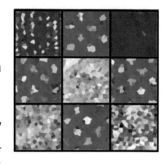

We love Nine-Patches, both to look at and to make.

Fussy-cut a 4½" x 4½" focus fabric square. Cut 4 squares 4½" x 4½" from 2 contrasting fabrics (8 total). (A variation we used in our quilt was to cut the last 4 squares from 2 different fabrics.)

Position the squares in a nine-patch arrangement of 3 rows of 3 blocks each with the focus fabric square in the center and the remaining squares alternated around it. Join the squares into rows. Press the top and bottom row seam allowances toward the ends, and press the center row seam allowances toward the center. Join the rows, nesting the seam allowances. Press.

Block 2 - Nine-Patch with Four-Patch Corners

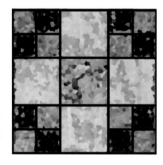

Make a strip-set with 2 strips 2½" x 21" cut from contrasting fabrics. Press the seam allowance toward the darker fabric. Cut 8 segments 2½" wide. Join 2 segments to make a four-patch unit. Make 4.

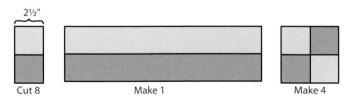

2½"

Cut 8   Make 1   Make 4

Fussy-cut a 4½" x 4½" focus fabric square and 4 squares 4½" x 4½" from a contrasting fabric.

Position the squares and four-patch units in a nine-patch arrangement with the four-patch units in the corners. Sew the squares into rows and sew the rows together as before.

Your second block is complete.

Block 3 - Log Cabin

Another fun and easy block!

Fussy-cut a 4½" x 4½" focus fabric square.

Choose 4 coordinating fabrics and label them A, B, C, and D.

From A, cut 2 strips 1½" x 4½" and 2 strips 1½" by 6½".
From B, cut 2 strips 1½" x 6½" and 2 strips 1½" x 8½".
From C, cut 2 strips 1½" x 8½" and 2 strips 1½" x 10½".
From D, cut 2 strips 1½" x 10½" and 2 strips 1½" by 12½".

In alphabetical order, stitch the 2 shorter strips to opposite sides of the center square. Then sew the 2 longer strips of the same fabric to the top and bottom. Press the seams away from the center throughout.

Another block to admire!

Block 4 - Nine-Patch with Half-Square Triangles

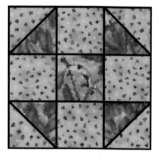

By now you must love Nine-Patches, too.

Fussy-cut a 4½" x 4½" focus fabric square.

To make the half-square triangles, cut 2 squares 5" x 5" from 2 contrasting fabrics (4 total). Draw a diagonal line, corner to corner, on the back of the 2 lighter squares.

Place the marked squares right sides together with the darker squares. Sew ¼" on both sides of the drawn line, cut on the line, and press open with the seam allowance toward the darker fabric. Trim each half-square triangle to measure 4½" x 4½", centering the diagonal seam.

Make 4

Cut 4 squares 4½" squares from a coordinating fabric.

Position the squares and half-square triangles in a nine-patch arrangement with the half-square triangles in the corners. Sew them into rows and sew the rows together as before.

Simply done and simply sensational!

Block 5 – Flying Geese Star 1

Fussy-cut a 4½" x 4½" focus fabric square.

For the flying geese units, cut 4 rectangles 2½" x 4½" from 2 different fabrics (A & B; 8 total); and 16 squares

2½" x 2½" from a highly contrasting fabric (C). Draw a diagonal line on the back of each square.

Align a square with the end of a rectangle, right sides together, with the drawn line positioned as shown. Stitch on the drawn line. Press the square back along the stitched line, forming a triangle. Trim the middle layer of fabric to ¼". In the same way, sew a

second square to the opposite end of the rectangle, positioning the drawn line in the opposite direction. Press and trim. Make 8 flying geese units.

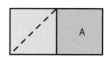

Sew along the drawn line   Make 8

Join pairs of 2 different flying geese units as shown.

Make 4

Cut 4 squares 4½" x 4½" from fabric B.

Position the focus fabric square, the plain squares, and flying geese units in a nine-patch arrangement, forming the star. Sew the squares into rows and sew the rows together as before.

Pretty fancy Nine-Patch!

Block 6 – Foundation Paper-Pieced Star

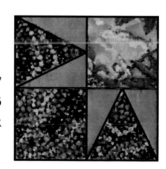

Fussy-cut a 6½" x 6½" focus fabric square. Cut 3 background squares 6½" x 6½".

For the star points, cut 4 rectangles 3¾" x 8". Trace 2 foundation paper-pieced (FPP) patterns (page 90) onto tracing paper.

Place a background square right-side up on the back of a FPP pattern. Fold the FPP back on one sewing line and trim the background fabric ¼" beyond the line. Align the 8" side of a rectangle with the cut edge of the background fabric, right sides together. Flip the FPP over and stitch on the sewing line. Press open.

Repeat for other side. Trim the unit to measure 6½" x 6½". Make 2.

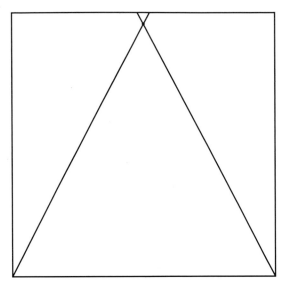

FPP for Block 6 – Star Points
Enlarge 200%

Position the star point units and squares in a four-patch arrangement. Sew them into rows and sew the rows together as before.

Wasn't this simple and really a WOW block?

Block 7 – Quarter-Square Star 1

The star points are constructed with quarter-square triangle units.

Fussy-cut a 4½" x 4½" focus fabric square.

Cut 2 squares 6" x 6" from a light fabric (A). Cut 1 square 6" x 6" from each of 2 darker fabrics (B & C; 2 total).

Make 2 half-square triangle units with fabrics A & B and 2 half-square triangle units with fabrics A & C (see Block 4 instructions, pages 88–89).

Draw a diagonal line on the back of the A/B units perpendicular to the seam. Place an A/B unit on top

of an A/C unit right sides together, with the seams matching but the darker fabrics opposite each other. Sew ¼" on each side of the line, cut on the line, and press open. Trim each quarter-square triangle unit to measure 4½" x 4½", centering the diagonal seam. Make 4.

Make 4

For the corner blocks, cut 4 rectangles 2½" x 4½" from fabric C; 4 squares 2½" x 2½" from fabric B; and 4 squares 2½" x 2½" from another fabric (D). Arrange as shown. Join the squares. Press, then add to the rectangles. Press.

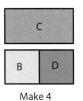

Make 4

Position the center block, quarter-square triangles, and corner squares in a nine-patch arrangement. Sew them into rows and sew the rows together as before.

Block 8 – Log Cabin

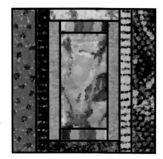

Fussy-cut a focus fabric square of a size of your choice ½" larger than your desired finished size.

Cut an assortment of complementary strips in a variety of widths. Add one at a time, going around the block in a clockwise direction, trimming the strips even with the block after each addition. Press the seam allowances away from the center square throughout.

When the block is larger than 12½" across, trim to measure 12½" x 12½".

Block 9 – Quarter-Square Star II

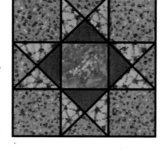

This is a simpler version of Block 7.

Fussy-cut a 4½" x 4½" focus fabric square.

Cut 2 squares 6" x 6" (A) and 1 square 6" x 6" from each of 2 different fabrics (B & C; total 2).

Cut 4 squares 4½" x 4½" from one of the same fabrics for the corners (C).

Refer to the Block 7 instructions (page 90) to make 4 quarter-square triangle units. Trim them to measure 4½" x 4½".

Position the center square, quarter-square triangles, and corner squares in a nine-patch arrangement. Sew them into rows and sew the rows together as before.

Block 10 – Log Cabin

Fussy-cut a 6" x 6" focus fabric square.

Sew three rounds of light and dark strips around the center square, adding them in a clockwise direction. Note the wider strips in the third round. Press the seam allowances away from the center square throughout.

Round	Top Light Strip	Right-Side Light Strip	Bottom Dark Strip	Left-Side Dark Strip
1	1½" x 6"	1½" x 7"	1½" x 7"	1½" x 8"
2	1½" x 8"	1½" x 9"	1½" x 9"	1½" x 10"
3	1¾" x 10"	1¾" x 11¼"	1¾" x 11¼"	1¾" x 12½"

Trim the block to measure 12½" x 12½".

Block 11 – Star in a Star

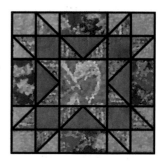

What a complicated look-ing block that is easy to construct! The star points are simply flying geese and half-square triangle units.

Fussy-cut a 4½" x 4½" focus fabric square.

For the inner star, cut
4 rectangles 2½" x 4½" from background fabric (A)
4 squares 2½" x 2½" from the same background fabric (A)
8 squares 2½" x 2½" from star point fabric (B)

Make 4 flying geese units (see Block 5 instructions, page 89). Set aside the background squares until you're ready to assemble the block.

For the outer star, cut
1 strip 3¼" x 13" from the star point fabric (B)
1 strip 3¼" x 13" from a second background fabric (C)

On the wrong side of the lighter of the strips, draw parallel lines 3¼" apart. Then draw diagonal lines as shown. Place the 2 strips right sides together and stitch ¼" on both sides of the diagonal lines as indicated by the dashed line.

Cut apart on the solid lines. Open and press toward the darker fabric. Trim to measure 2½" x 2½", centering the diagonal seam.

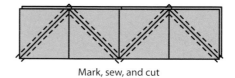

Mark, sew, and cut 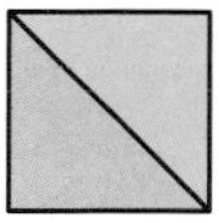   Make 8

From the second background fabric (C) cut 4 squares 2½" x 2½".

From a different fabric (D) cut 4 rectangles 2½" x 4½".

Arrange the center squares, flying geese units, half-square triangle units, and corner squares as shown. Sew them into 5 rows and sew the rows together as before.

Block 12 – Friendship Star

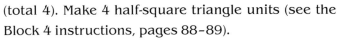

Fussy-cut a 4½" x 4½" focus fabric square.

Cut 2 squares each 5" x 5" from 2 contrasting fabrics (total 4). Make 4 half-square triangle units (see the Block 4 instructions, pages 88–89).

Cut 4 squares 4½" x 4½" from a third, coordinating fabric.

Arrange the half-square triangle units and squares in a nine-patch arrangement. Sew them into rows and sew the rows together as before.

Sashing and Cornerstones

From the purple fabric, cut
     12 strips 1½" x 40" (width of fabric)
     1 strip 2" x 20"

From the green fabric, cut
     6 strips 2" x 40"
     2 strips 1½" x 20"

Make 6 strip-sets with the 40" long strips and 1 strip-set with the 20" strips, with the wide strips in the middle. Press all the seam allowances toward the purple.

Cut 17 segments 12½" wide and 6 segments 2" wide from the 40" strip-sets.

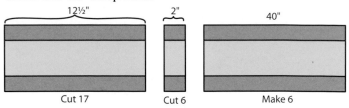

Cut 12 segments 1½" wide from the 20" strip-set.

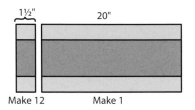

Make 6 cornerstones with the 1½" and 2" segments. Press the seam allowances toward the middle.

Make 6

Arrange the blocks in 4 rows of 3 blocks each, leaving about 4" between the blocks. Fill in the spaces with the sashing units and cornerstones as shown.

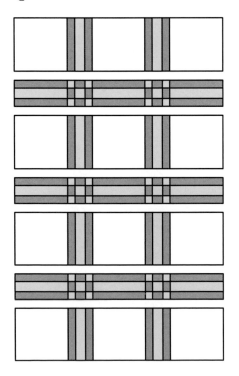

Sew 4 rows of blocks and sashing units and 3 rows of sashing units and cornerstones. Press all the seam allowances toward the sashing units. Sew the rows together, nesting the seam allowances.

Border

From the purple fabric, cut
> 12 strips 2" x 40"
> 1 strip 3" x 40"
> 1 strip 3" x 20"
> 1 strip 2" x 20"

From the green fabric, cut
> 6 strips 3" x 40"
> 1 strip 3" x 20"
> 1 strip 2" x 40"
> 1 strip 2" x 20"

Make 6 strip-sets 40" long with the wider green strips in the center. Press the seam allowances toward the purple.

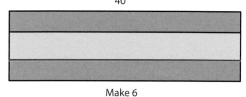

40"

Make 6

Cut:
> 14 segments 12½" wide
> 4 segments 3" wide
> 10 segments 2" wide

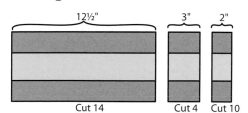

12½"   3"   2"

Cut 14   Cut 4   Cut 10

Make 1 strip-set 40" long and 1 strip-set 20" long, each with the wider purple strip in the center. Press the seam allowances toward the purple.

Cut 8 segments 2" wide and 20 segments 1½" wide.

Make 1–40" and 1–20" strip-set

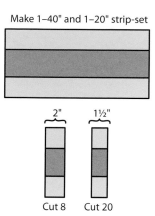

2"   1½"

Cut 8   Cut 20

Make 10 border nine-patch units with the 1½" and 2" segments as shown.

Make 4 corner nine-patch units with the 2" and 3" segments as shown.

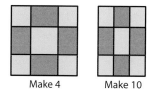

Make 4   Make 10

Join 3 border nine-patch units and 4 of the 12½" segments for the side borders. Make 2. Add to the sides of the quilt top, nesting the seam allowances.

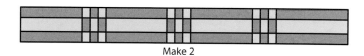

Make 2

Join 2 border nine-patch units, 3 of the 12½" segments, and 2 corner nine-patch units for the top and bottom borders. Make 2. Add to the top and bottom of the quilt, nesting the seam allowances.

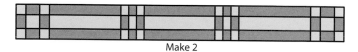

Make 2

Can you believe it? Your quilt top is now ready to be quilted so some wonderful child will be able to cuddle up in all the love you've invested in making this beauty. We simply quilted ours "in the ditch."

CHOCOLATE DREAMS by Jan Lawhorn, Fort Wayne, Indiana. Notice how Jan embellished each block. Her quilt has great appeal from a distance, and is even more fun to study up-close.

And just who are those Crafty Ol' Broads?

Jane and Linda are sisters who have a passion for just about everything to do with quilting and who love sharing their knowledge and enthusiasm. They are award-winning quilters who also are crafty, old, and broad! (Jane's older, Linda's broader.)

Both started quilting in 2001 and before they had their first quilts done, they were excitedly designing their own quilts in their sleep as well as during their waking hours.

Linda and her husband, Gary, are the proud parents of five grown children with five grandkids. Linda is happy to say that they all have at least one of her quilts to cuddle in. When she isn't quilting or playing with her grandkids, Linda enjoys gardening and is very active in her community and church. Her sense of humor and natural warmth make her one of those people who doesn't know a stranger.

Jane has seven grown children and stepchildren and thirteen grandchildren. Most are happy owners of her quilts and a few are making their own quilts with Jane's guidance. Jane loves hiking on her farm with her dogs and caring for her llamas and reindeer. She derives great joy from her gardens, but the thing that gives her the greatest pleasure is playing with her grandkids.

These sisters live about a half an hour apart, but they talk almost daily and manage to get together every week or two to share their latest ideas and creations. As "the Crafty Ol' Broads," Linda and Jane teach all levels of quilting, travel for lectures and classes, design and sell their patterns, and import and sell handwoven Guatemalan fabric. Visit their Web site at www.craftyolbroads.com.

"We'd love to hear from you. Share your quilt photos with us."

Jane K. Wells
wellswildnwooly@aol.com
Fort Wayne, Indiana

Linda K. Johnson
lindajohnson07@verizon.net
Monroeville, Indiana

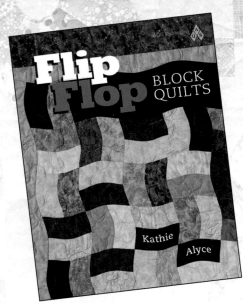

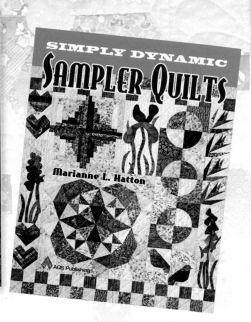

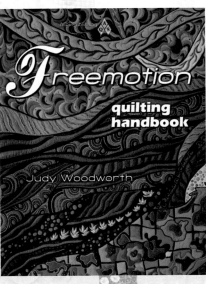